MORE PRAISE FO..
Surviving Your Bar/Bat Mitzvah: The Ultimate Insider's Guide

"In an age when the 'bar' seems to have eclipsed 'mitzvah,' it's more important than ever for parents to instill a strong sense of faith and identity. Grab this book! You'll be doing your kid(s) a favor."

— **Rabbi Simcha Weinstein, author of *Up, Up, and Oy Vey: How Jewish History, Culture, and Values Shaped the Comic Book Hero***

"Cantor Matt Axelrod has written an easily accessible guide for both parents and kids that will help anyone to have a successful bar or bat mitzvah experience with the least stress possible."

— **Rabbi Steven Carr Reuben, author of *Becoming Jewish: The Challenges, Rewards, and Paths to Conversion***

"Engaging from the first sentence and jam-packed with relevant information, Cantor Axelrod's book is a wonderful roadmap for both parents and kids. Axelrod is that rare grown-up who has joyously retained the spirit of a big kid, albeit one with 'insider' information. He addresses everything from the structure of the service to the adolescent terror of embarrassment and public attention. The result is a book that makes you wonder, 'What did parents and kids do without a book like this?!'"

— **Dr. Elizabeth Arnold, clinical psychologist specializing in adolescents**

Surviving YOUR Bar/Bat Mitzvah

THE ULTIMATE INSIDER'S GUIDE

Cantor Matt Axelrod

JASON ARONSON

Lanham • Boulder • New York • Toronto • Plymouth, UK

Published by Jason Aronson
A wholly owned subsidiary of The Rowman & Littlefield Publishing Group, Inc.
4501 Forbes Boulevard, Suite 200, Lanham, Maryland 20706
www.rowman.com

10 Thornbury Road, Plymouth PL6 7PP, United Kingdom

British Library Cataloguing in Publication Information Available

Library of Congress Cataloging-in-Publication Data
Axelrod, Cantor Matt, 1966–
    Surviving your bar/bat mitzvah : the ultimate insider's guide / Cantor Matt Axelrod.
        p. cm.
    Includes index.
    ISBN 978-0-7657-0887-8 (pbk. : alk. paper) —
    ISBN 978-0-7657-0888-5 (electronic)
    1. Bar mitzvah. 2. Bat mitzvah. I. Title.
BM707.A94 2012
296.4'424—dc23   2012007071

Printed in the United States of America

For Tali

Contents

CONTENTS

Acknowledgments

"**H**EY, I'VE got a great idea for a book!"
Little did I know how much effort it would involve to transform that thought into the finished product you're holding in your hands. I want to express my gratitude to the many people without whom it would not have been possible. First I'd like to thank my agent, Anne Devlin, for her advice and persistence. This project would never have proceeded without her. Thank you to my editor, Julie Kirsch, and her assistant, Lindsey Porambo. Julie's expertise and enormous patience with a novice author were remarkable, and I can't imagine how she was able to restrain herself from finally breaking into my home and ripping out the comma key from my computer keyboard. Many thanks to David Barash for his funny cartoons that appear throughout this book.

An enormous thank you goes out to my friends at Congregation Beth Israel of Scotch Plains, New Jersey. I can't believe how fortunate I am to have been able to call this synagogue my home for more than twenty years, and I appreciate the warmth, humor, and support I get every time I walk into the building. And finally, of course, none of this would have been possible without the love and patience of my wife Tali and my sons Judah and Josh. They have enjoyed taking this adventure with me every step of the way and weren't shy about letting me know when a joke I wrote wasn't as funny as I thought. Thanks for always being there.

Introduction

WHO DOESN'T love having a guy on the inside?

Imagine that it's your first day at a new school and you have no idea where anything is. Suddenly another student comes along and explains how to navigate the corridors. He tells you how to find your classrooms and to take a certain way because you'll avoid all the kids coming out of the cafeteria after lunch and make much faster progress. And when he learns that you have Mrs. Jones for English, he lets you know that if you just memorize the answers to the chapter review questions, you'll ace every test, but you should be careful because she always takes points off for spelling mistakes.

Parents, pretend that you're booking a hotel in some distant location. All the rooms sound nice, but the manager of the hotel calls you up and tells you to stay away from a certain wing because you'll be bothered by traffic noise, and instead to take a corner room on the eighth floor in another location because the rooms were just renovated.

Everyone loves getting inside information.

Consider me *your* guy on the inside.

So how did the whole bar mitzvah thing start? I imagine the scene went something like this:

One day, God was holding a meeting with His entire board of angel VPs, and they were sitting around a big conference table. God came to the next order of business on that day's agenda—when and how to start requiring Jews to begin observing the rituals and commandments.

One angel, the VP in Charge of Romance and Nuptials, suggested that once a Jewish person got married and moved out of the house, that would mark the time when he would start being responsible. God brought up the very good point that not everyone gets married, or, for that matter, moves out of the house.

A second angel who was the VP in Charge of Self-Esteem and Free-thinking stated that he always thought it best for people to make their own decisions. According to him, each Jew should have the right to decide whenever they think they're ready to start observing the commandments of the Jewish religion.

Then the VP in Charge of Growth and Hormones raised his wing and said, "I've got it. Let's take young people when they're about thirteen years old. It's perfect. They're just starting to go through puberty, their voices are changing, and they're socially awkward and self-conscious. We'll make them stand up in front of all their friends and family and sing for hours. Plus, they'll have to do it in another language."

The room got very quiet as everyone looked around. Suddenly God announced, "Splendid idea!" Of course, there was no vote; when the Almighty makes a decision, that's that.

God dismissed the gathering and rushed off to His next meeting. After He left, the VP looked around and very sheepishly said, "Actually, I was joking."

But now we're stuck with it, and you will have to take your turn in front of the congregation, singing, bowing, chanting, reading, and doing lots of other things that you could never imagine. And your parents will have to not only see you through the whole thing, but also deal with a ton of other chores as well.

Will it be too much to handle? How will you ever learn *so* much material and prepare it well enough to sing in front of a couple hundred of your closest friends and relatives? What if you mess up? How about if you've never gone to services before? What should you do if you don't believe in God and think the whole thing doesn't make sense to you? How can you fit practicing in with your already busy schedule of homework, after-school activities, and sports?

Parents are often just as mystified and nervous about what their kids have to do and their role in this whole process. Sometimes, you're made to feel guilty or vaguely lacking as a parent if you don't know as much as everyone else or have a lot of questions. This book is for you too.

I'll address all those questions and sensitive issues, and much more. This is not a spiritual guide to the Jewish religion. Nor will I bore you with useless imagine-the-audience-in-their-underwear type of advice, although given the way that dress codes have changed nowadays, maybe that's not so hard to do. Instead, this is a book that you can use *right now.*

In addition, like any good inside guy, I'll let you know what you *don't* have to worry about, and which advice you can ignore. You'll also find special sections titled *Insider's Tip!* and *Just for Parents* that will go even deeper. This book should be shared and passed back and forth between bar mitzvah student and parents.

You'll find the information inside incredibly useful no matter what kind of synagogue you attend. Whether your temple is Conservative or Reform, huge or intimate, the advice in this book will be invaluable. It also is intended equally for boys and girls. You can easily substitute "bar" and "bat" for each other any time you like, and the advice and information will never change.

In my over twenty years of being a cantor and teaching nervous students, I have never lost a bar mitzvah kid yet, and I promise you there's no way you'll be the first. So take a deep breath, and get ready to have some fun. . . .

Why Am I Having a Bar or Bat Mitzvah?

SO YOU'VE decided to have a bar or bat mitzvah!

OK, maybe you didn't exactly decide yourself. Maybe your parents told you what's in your future, or you belong to a synagogue, and you just know by a certain time, this is what's supposed to happen.

You may be looking forward to the big day with enthusiasm, with unbridled terror, or some combination of the two.

What *is* this thing they call *bar mitzvah*?

The Background

The term *bar mitzvah* literally means "son of the commandments," and *bat mitzvah* is "daughter of the commandments." There, that was helpful, right?

Let's start again. What in the world does son or daughter of the commandments mean?

It's actually pretty simple. It just means that you are now of the age where you are expected to observe the *mitzvot* (commandments) and other rituals of the Jewish tradition. Here's an easy example: You know that people fast on Yom Kippur. You probably also know that little kids don't. (Can you imagine telling a five-year-old that he can't eat again for twenty-four hours? "Now go run along and play. Dinner will be in a couple of days.")

Well, when does that little kid have to start fasting for real? You got it—after her bat mitzvah. As of that date, she's considered, at least when talking about Jewish laws, the same as a grownup.

Here's a little grammar quiz for you, because I *love* grammar: What part of speech is the term *bar mitzvah*?

Maybe it's a noun. That would certainly make sense.

"I went to a bar mitzvah the other day." "We're planning her bat mitzvah."

How about a verb?

"He was bar mitzvahed a month ago." "Can I hold the Torah? I was never bat mitzvahed."

Wrong and wronger.

The term *bar mitzvah* is an adjective! I bet you've never used it that way before and can't even picture what I'm talking about. Here's a proper use of the term:

"Because she is bat mitzvah now, she can lead part of the service."

If you insert the words "of age" in place of the term *bat mitzvah*, it all makes more sense. Kids can and should do a lot of things in *shul* (synagogue) after they turn thirteen and become bar mitzvah (that is, after they become a certain age).

Putting the suffix "ed" on bar mitzvah has always amused me. It makes me picture a giant machine with lots of tubes and hoses, smoke coming from the top, and a lot of clanging noise. A thirteen-year-old kid walks into this machine, at which point it starts to chug and huff and make a noisy racket. Finally, it all stops, and out he walks, with a new suit and uplifted face. He's been . . . *bar mitzvahed*!!!

Or sometimes at my synagogue, which is egalitarian (meaning we treat men and women exactly the same—more on that later), we will often ask women to come up for an *aliyah* to the Torah (a kind of honor). Every now and then someone might respond, "Oh, thank you, but I can't, because I was never bat mitzvahed."

Here's the real story:

As soon as a boy or girl turns thirteen according to the Jewish calendar (which I'll explain in much more detail in chapter 4), that kid has become bar or bat mitzvah. (Remember using the word like an adjective?) Even if you never did a single thing, never learned a letter of Hebrew, and even if you went out for a ham and cheese sandwich on Yom Kippur (kids, don't try this), you would still be bar mitzvah.

Look at it this way:

In this country, when you turn twenty-one, you're allowed to order a drink in a bar. (Sorry, parents, this is the best example I could come up with.) There's no ceremony to celebrate that, except perhaps on certain college campuses, but I digress. Hopefully, sometime before your twenty-first birthday, your parents had a talk with you about responsible drinking. Maybe you attended assemblies in high school discussing the dangers of drinking and driving. You may have joined Students Against Drunk Driving. Finally, you may have decided that you're just not interested in drinking at all because you hate the taste.

But one way or the other, when you wake up on the morning of your twenty-first birthday, you are allowed to drink certain beverages, because our society assumes that you are responsible enough by that age to handle the risks and consequences. There's no such thing as being *drinking aged*, just like you don't become *bar mitzvahed*.

Therefore, when you open your eyes and stumble out of bed on the morning after your thirteenth birthday, you are bar mitzvah. It is as simple as that. Technically, you don't need some huge, expensive ceremony. You already got there just by living long enough.

So if all that is true (and it is—I use a fact checker), then what is the deal with the bar mitzvah ceremony?

To answer that question, we need to go back in time to olden days. So cue the flashback music, pretend the screen is getting all wavy, and imagine this next part in black and white. . . .

Back in the days when men were men, and women cooked for them, a boy and his father would regularly go to the synagogue each Shabbat morning. The father would put on a *tallit* (prayer shawl) and the boy would try to follow along in the service, and spend a lot of time hoping that lunch was coming up pretty soon. Maybe Dad got called up to the Torah for an *aliyah*, but the boy wouldn't, because he wasn't old enough. It's also possible that Dad was asked to lead part of the service, but Junior wasn't able to, even if he knew all the words and melodies, because he wasn't old enough yet.

Then, one beautiful morning, our happy family realized that the boy had just passed his thirteenth birthday in the Jewish calendar. Well, next

"But Dad, why do I need a bar mitzvah? I'm not exempt?!"

Shabbat would be different. At the next Shabbat service, the boy would be able to lead part of the service, if so requested, or to have an *aliyah* if asked.

Actually, why leave it to chance? This was a big deal. Therefore, at the service, the guys handing out the honors made sure to give the boy an *aliyah*. This would be his very first one! And when he was done, everyone congratulated him. And following the service, everyone had some *schnapps* and made a *l'chayim*. (I'm too tired to translate all that—go find a grandparent.)

Nowadays we sort of do it backward. In a lot of households, the ceremony gets planned first, and the religious part is an afterthought.

The Service

So let's talk about what a basic service might be like to celebrate a boy or girl becoming bar mitzvah or bat mitzvah. Remember that when I use a term in Hebrew, you can always look it up in the glossary in the back of the book.

Bear in mind the most important thing. Before you even sing a note, put on your suit, or open a single check, *you are already bar mitzvah!* The

INSIDER'S TIP!

THERE'S AN old joke that says if you put three Jews in a room, you get four opinions. If you don't believe this is true, consider the fact that we can't even agree on what to call our places of worship!

The best term to describe where Jews gather to pray is "synagogue." Many people also say "temple," and in fact, this word might actually appear in your synagogue's name (like "Temple Beth El" or "Temple Shalom").

But some Jews who are more religious balk at using the word "temple," since it reminds them of the Temple (capital T) that stood in Jerusalem a couple thousand years ago. There were actually two Temples at different times in history—each was destroyed. Our tradition teaches that only when the Messiah comes will there be a Third Temple. Calling our place of worship a "temple" contradicts this, so they don't like to use that term.

You may have heard the word *shul*. This is actually a Yiddish word meaning synagogue, and is used very commonly especially by Jews of a certain generation. This happens to be my favorite term because it's quick and easy, and doesn't sound as formal as "synagogue."

The bottom line is that you can use any of these words, and I will use them interchangeably throughout the book.

service and all the stuff you'll end up doing are there to help commemorate your new adult status in the Jewish community.

Don't get me wrong. I'm not saying that the bar mitzvah service and all of the preparation that goes along with it isn't important. Rather, you should just understand that nothing magical happens during the course of the service. You don't walk into the temple that morning, participate in the service, and leave as a magically changed person.

All of your hard work and learning reflect the fact that you are now ready to start taking some responsibility for the Jewish laws and traditions.

Who Wants to Be a Minyanaire?

First and foremost, when a child turns thirteen, he or she may now be counted in a *minyan*.

JUST FOR PARENTS

WHAT **EXACTLY** is the plural of bar mitzvah?

Well, you could just add an S, as in "I've written so many checks for my son's friends' bar mitzvahs that I'm broke!"

Some people know that the plural form of the Hebrew word *mitzvah* is mitzvot. So they figure that if there's one bar mitzvah, then there are many bar mitzvot.

But wait—the term "bar" doesn't refer to the place where everyone immediately heads when the party starts, but rather to the words "son of." And for a girl, the word "bat" means "daughter of." So the plural forms of those words would be b'nei (sons of) and b'not (daughters of). If you put it all together, you then have b'nei mitzvot and b'not mitzvot as the two plural forms, which is what a lot of people say.

They're wrong!

Think of the term "mother-in-law." (And if you're already planning who has to get honors during the service, you're way ahead of me.) The plural is "mothers-in-law." It works the same way in our case. The plural of bar mitzvah is b'nei mitzvah, and bat mitzvah becomes b'not mitzvah.

Ready for extra credit? What do you say if you're trying to refer to both boys and girls? Look for the answer at the end of this chapter.

Simply put, a *minyan* refers to ten or more Jewish adults. (Remember that a *Jewish adult* means thirteen or older.) Many of the prayers that are recited in the service may only be done when there's a *minyan* present. Imagine if you were running a club, and you called a big meeting to make important decisions for your group. It wouldn't be very productive if only a few members showed up. In fact, you might go one step further and decide that unless you had a minimum number of people attending your meeting, you wouldn't be able to vote at all. Real organizations do this all the time by requiring a quorum, a certain number of people that must be present. A *minyan,* then, is a Jewish version of a quorum.

Of course, we now start wading into treacherous waters, as we try to get more specific: Does our *minyan* have to be all male? How do you know if someone is Jewish? Do we count someone who was never bat mitzvahed? (groan . . .)

JUST FOR PARENTS

IT'S HARD to imagine that your cute little thirteen-year-old is an adult, and for good reason! It's not true, notwithstanding the old cliché "Today I am a man!" that the kid in every movie or TV show always says.

It does remind me of one of my favorite stories: One Monday afternoon in my synagogue the previous weekend's bar mitzvah boy saw me and yelled all the way down the temple corridor: "CANTOR, I'M A MAN NOW!"

I thought to myself, "Wow, that must have been some party."

The Jewish religion set a line in the sand (probably while they were wandering in the desert) and said: If you're younger than *this*, you are exempt from certain obligations. If you're *this* age, then you must perform them. And the age of thirteen was the magic number. Sure, it undoubtedly harkens back to a time when the average thirteen-year-old had a lot more responsibilities in the family—farming, earning money, and working around the house.

Our ancestors most likely didn't envision a time when turning thirteen meant you might be mature enough for your own cell phone.

Depending on whom you ask, or which synagogue you're in, you will get various answers to these questions, and therefore a different definition of the very meaning of *minyan*.

An Orthodox Jew would only count males, but that doesn't matter much for our subject, since a girl probably wouldn't have a bat mitzvah in an Orthodox synagogue anyway.

Why is it so important to be counted in a *minyan*? After all, isn't there usually a big crowd that attends services?

Sometimes yes, other times . . . not so much.

Yes, on the day of your bar mitzvah, you'll probably be expecting a lot of invited family and friends, and the question of some minimum number of Jews who are present will not be an issue.

But there are many other situations where *you*, the brand-new Jewish adult, can and will make all the difference. Many synagogues have daily or

INSIDER'S TIP!

WHY IS it less common for a girl to become bat mitzvah in an Orthodox community? Why don't women count in a *minyan* in an Orthodox synagogue?

There are many laws and commandments in the Jewish religion, and many of them are what we call "time-bound," meaning that they must be performed at a certain time and in a specific place.

For instance, Jews are supposed to pray three times a day—called *Shacharit* (morning service), *Mincha* (afternoon service), and *Ma'ariv* (evening service). Back in "olden" times (way before the Internet), women usually stayed home and took care of the house, were pregnant a lot of the time, and remained busy running after lots of little kids. It wasn't a lifestyle choice that women of that time made—it was just the way things were.

Consequently, Jewish law decided that it would be unfair and downright impossible to require women to get to services and pray at those times when they constantly had their hands full with those other very important responsibilities. So women became exempt from performing these and certain other *mitzvot* (commandments).

As other branches of Judaism came along and developed, such as Reform and Conservative, they saw that the role of women in society had evolved, and that Judaism's expectations of them should similarly change. So in Reform as well as most Conservative congregations, women are completely integrated into all aspects of Temple leadership and service participation.

A congregation that holds these views is referred to as an *egalitarian* congregation, meaning they consider men and women to be equal participants in Jewish laws and rituals.

Sunday morning services in addition to the biggies on Shabbat and festivals. Because these are usually less formal, and much more lightly attended, there are often times when there might only be about ten people there.

Earlier, I mentioned that some prayers may only be recited in the service if there is a *minyan* present. One of those prayers, and in fact one of the most famous ones, is the Mourners' Kaddish. This is a prayer that is recited by a worshipper who is mourning the death of a family member sometime within the past year. It is also said every year after that on the anniversary

INSIDER'S TIP!

Let's see, can we make things any more confusing for you? I know, let's take a word that you just learned—*minyan*—and give you yet another meaning for it.

In many cases, the word *minyan* refers to the actual service itself where you would want the *minyan* present.

Huh?

If you have a small, informal service, you might refer to that as a *minyan*. For instance, one could say, "I have to get up early because *minyan* begins at 7 am." Note that we don't use this word when talking about a large service, like on Shabbat morning, or maybe Rosh Hashanah. Is there a magic cutoff: less than a certain size and it's a *minyan*, but bigger than that and it's a service? No—you just know when it's a *minyan*.

And just to have some more fun, if you take both meanings and use them at the same time, you can come up with some pretty crazy sentences:

"I went to the *minyan* where I hoped there'd be a *minyan*, but there wasn't a *minyan* at the *minyan*."

Translation:

"I went to the small service where I hoped there'd be ten people, but there weren't ten people at the service."

of the family member's death. As you can imagine, it can become rather emotional for the person saying it out loud. Many Jews come to services just because they know that they have to recite the Kaddish.

Now picture the scene when there are only nine people who showed up.

That's right—the Kaddish is not recited. The Mourners' Kaddish is not a prayer *for* the person who passed away, but rather a declaration of faith by the surviving family member, who stands up in public and recites words that praise God. The word "public" is the key here. If there's no *minyan* present, then it's not considered to be public prayer, and we would skip that page.

That can be pretty upsetting to the person who came just because she wanted to say the Kaddish.

Here's where you come in: As a Jewish adult now, you can help make sure that there are enough people to say not only the Kaddish but all the other important prayers that require a *minyan* be present. You can play your part by coming to services whenever possible. (And if you force your parents to drive you there, that's even more people who showed up!)

The Torah

Many services revolve around reading the Torah.

If the Torah is that big, fancy scroll that's kept in the ark, then what exactly is the haftarah? Where does it appear?

The Torah is also known as the Five Books of Moses, and you probably already know the name of at least some of these books: Genesis, Exodus, Leviticus, Numbers, and Deuteronomy. I further predict that pretty much any biblical episode or character that you can think of would be found somewhere in these five very important books. (Adam and Eve, Noah, Abraham, Sarah, Isaac, Jacob, Joseph and his brothers, Moses, Aaron, Pharaoh, Splitting of the Red Sea, Ten Commandments . . . they're all right there in the Torah.)

Of course, since they are referred to as the Five Books of *Moses,* it helps to remember that they all end with Moses' death—sad, but it sure makes sense.

That means that everything else that happened throughout Jewish history took place after the Torah. There were many additional important characters that followed, and many of them were prophets—that is, they heard and communicated the word of God. (If anyone said they could do that today, they'd be locked up!)

So after the Torah, we have a whole section called *Prophets.* And it's from this section that every haftarah is taken. Your haftarah might come from a book called Isaiah, or Ezekiel, or even Habakkuk! (You just know that poor prophet was teased really badly when he was a kid.) These guys were all prophets and have books named after them.

Each week we read a portion (or in Hebrew, *parsha*) of Torah. Generally, these go in order from the beginning of the Torah all the way through to the end as we progress through the entire year. And each of these weekly Torah portions has a haftarah assigned to it—always the same one for each specific *parsha.* Usually there's some connection between the subject of the Torah portion and its haftarah.

When we read from the Torah, we usually do it right out of the scroll, which is written in a fancy calligraphy and doesn't have any vowels or punctuation. (At which point you blurt out, "Then how do I read it?!" More on that later, but in the meantime, trust me, you *can* do it!) The haftarah doesn't appear in the Torah scroll, so that is read with vowels and other markings. You'll probably have your own copy of the haftarah that you can mark up and make helpful notations for yourself—and then use that same copy at your bar mitzvah service. Sweet!

To help make the Torah reading special, we call up members of the congregation or others who are in attendance to make a blessing over the Torah, and then to listen while a portion is being read. This is called an *aliyah*.

On Shabbat, which is when most b'nei mitzvah are held, there are seven such *aliyot* (yup, you guessed it: plural). Depending on the specific policies of your temple, your family will have the opportunity to hand out some, or maybe all, of these *aliyot* to guests of your choosing—usually close relatives or friends.

Remember when I told you there are seven *aliyot* on Shabbat? Well, I sort of lied. (Sorry about that.) There is an additional *aliyah* that we add

JUST FOR PARENTS

THE ALIYAH blessings are probably one of the most well-known (and most butchered) texts in the entire service. You will almost surely be singing these at your child's service, as will any relatives and friends that you give this honor to.

Nothing . . . nothing! . . . cries out "amateur hour" more than someone who struggles and mangles his or her way through the text. And there's no need for it—in every synagogue I've ever been in, the blessings are displayed next to the Torah in large print and transliterated in English phonetic pronunciation as well. They're readily available online or through any synagogue, and I predict any cantor or rabbi would be happy to steer you in the right direction to prepare this very short and easy solo.

after the seven have finished, and it has a special name. (No, it's not called "eight." That would make way too much sense.) This mysterious post-seven-but-not-really-eighth *aliyah* is called *maftir,* and the person who gets honored with the *maftir aliyah* gets to stick around after the Torah reading is finished and do some more singing.

This lucky person gets to chant the haftarah. In many cases and depending on your temple, that's you.

Because you're thirteen now—that is, you're bar mitzvah—your congregation wants to honor you with something that you haven't been able to have until now—your own *aliyah.* Notice how you're already bar mitzvah before you actually receive the *aliyah* and chant any blessings. Remember—there's no magic machine, no angels singing, no shining light from above (unless you have a skylight in your sanctuary) to turn you into something new. You did just fine by living long enough to turn thirteen.

But since you're already getting an *aliyah* to commemorate this important day, why not go one step further and have the synagogue give *you* the *maftir?* After all, in many shuls, the *maftir aliyah* is reserved for someone important—perhaps a prominent member of the congregation or a visiting scholar. Today, you get to be the VIP.

INSIDER'S TIP!

THE WORD *haftarah* is often pronounced "HafTORah," leading many Jews to ask, "What is it, half the Torah?"

In fact, the Hebrew words *Torah* and *haftarah* (with the proper emphasis on the last syllable: haftaRAH) are not related at all, even though they look and sound so much alike and come so close to each other in the service. This little quirk of the Hebrew language has probably resulted in lots of confusion.

The word *Torah* comes from a Hebrew root meaning "teachings," while *haftarah* means "closing," as in the part which closes out the Torah service. I will consistently use the Hebrew-friendly spelling of haftarah to help minimize the confusion, and you might consider saying the word this way too.

So there you have it. Sure, undoubtedly you'll have to do a lot more—probably lead parts of the service, read from the Torah, and give some kind of speech—but these are all in addition to the basic premise of celebrating a young person becoming bar mitzvah by honoring him with his very first *aliyah.*

Answer to the extra credit question on page 10: You still say "b'nei mitzvah" even if you're talking about ninety-nine girls and even just one boy!

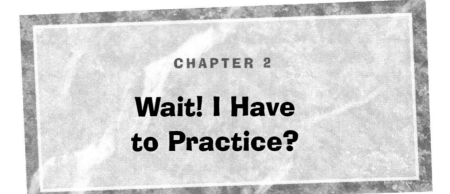

CHAPTER 2

Wait! I Have to Practice?

YES, YOU have to practice. OK, next chapter.

Oh wait, I suppose I should tell you more.

There are many different ways a person can think about the bar mitzvah from start to finish.

You may consider it an ordeal. After all, your non-Jewish friends don't have to deal with any of this. And parents, you might be thinking similar thoughts about your non-Jewish friends and neighbors who are putting many thousands of dollars into college savings accounts rather than in the hands of caterers and banquet halls. Hardly seems fair, does it?

Perhaps the word "ordeal" is a little strong for you, but you might regard it as a burden or at least a major hassle. All the schlepping to and from temple, making room in your weekly schedule for lessons (which probably means having to give up some activity), and preparing to sing in front of all those people. Meanwhile, Mom and Dad are frenetic with invitations, suit or dress shopping, and numerous financial and logistical arrangements.

Then there's the very real issue of peer pressure. I'm not using that phrase in a negative way, as if all your friends are doing something bad and you feel obligated to go along. In fact, it's just the opposite. All of your friends will be attending your bar mitzvah, just like you'll be a guest at all of theirs; the pressure will be on you not to do anything that you think will be embarrassing. Parents, by the way, are going through the same thing—it's very common for normal and secure adults to get caught up in the bar mitzvah frenzy and want to make sure that the service and party are successful and at a level comparable to all the other ones held that year.

Let me give you another perspective.

One of the most important things I look for in a successful bar mitzvah student is the ability to be independent, which I'll discuss more in chapter 10. While it's certainly positive for parents to be involved with and aware of their kids' lessons and progress, I think that this is a job mainly for the bar mitzvah student.

Big picture time. Remember that the most important goal, the ultimate result of celebrating your bar mitzvah, is to demonstrate that you are beginning to assume responsibility for your own life. Sure, that doesn't mean a lot when you're thirteen. You're still a kid and will be treated like one for a long time. That's why I said "beginning" to assume responsibility.

In our modern times, reaching age thirteen doesn't give you any independence. While Judaism may consider you responsible for and obligated to perform the commandments and rituals, your parents are still making the decisions. It's not like you can come to services if no one in your house is willing to attend or at least drive you to temple. Similarly, if your parents keep a kosher home, I wouldn't advise you to walk into your kitchen with a BLT. We rabbis and cantors love to say that you're a Jewish adult now, but really? Not so much.

It's perfectly OK to view your bar mitzvah as an obligation. It's like a hurdle you have to climb over on your way through being thirteen. There's nothing wrong with that. In fact, you're going to have *many, many* more hurdles to overcome after the bar mitzvah is over. How are you going to deal with them? Start thinking about that right now.

There's nothing in the world more satisfying than looking back on a job well done. Well, almost. The best feeling is remembering how much work you did and how hard it was. I know, I know—it sounds really corny. Stay with me here.

By this time in school, you've undoubtedly been assigned some big paper or assignment. If you had your choice, you probably wouldn't have volunteered to do all that work, but it was homework, so you had to get it done. Sometimes you can complete the assignment without too much effort, and other times . . . whoa, you go to sleep worrying about how you're going to finish it, if you're doing it right, and what grade you'll get. Maybe you had to stay up later than normal just to have enough time to finish your work.

Now, skip ahead to when you get your grade back in school. Congratulations, you got an A! I challenge you to disagree with me that the *harder you worked, the better you felt.* You'll want to wave that A around and tell everyone, "Oh my God, you should have seen how much work I did!" That is a great feeling—adults get like that too.

Your bar mitzvah can be the same way. So yes, you have to practice. But why not treat this as another really important assignment that you have. Just like a school project, you'll have materials, deadlines, and due dates, as well as opportunities to get extra help if you need it.

Your Teacher

Before you can even think about doing a huge assignment, you have to know who your teacher is, and that will actually depend on your specific temple and its policies.

Often, you will have lessons with your cantor or rabbi. Some temples don't employ a full-time cantor (a pity for them), so you may meet with the rabbi or another tutor who was hired for just this purpose. Your lessons may be thirty minutes every week, or maybe an hour. Again, this all has to do with how many kids your synagogue has to prepare each year and how much material you have to learn.

At some shuls, the rabbi is not directly involved in bar mitzvah tutoring, leaving the task for other professionals in the temple. Or you may meet with the rabbi for just a few sessions closer to your bar mitzvah date in order to run through things and possibly work on a speech or *d'var Torah* (a short explanation of the Torah reading or haftarah for that week). Whether it's your rabbi, cantor, b'nei mitzvah tutor, or even a high school or college student hired by the temple, different teachers bring diverse approaches to lessons.

The Materials

Most likely at your first lesson, you'll be given some different books or folders. First, there's your haftarah.

In some temples, you'll get a little booklet which contains the haftarah for your week, along with the blessings that are recited with it, and maybe an English translation of the text. The booklet might also contain information about trope symbols (*way* more about that in the next chapter), or a more detailed commentary on what your haftarah is about and how it relates to the Torah portion.

INSIDER'S TIP!

IN THE LAST chapter I explained the difference between the terms Torah and haftarah, but let's take a more complete look. Since you'll hear these terms very often throughout your bar mitzvah preparation, it's best if you really understand exactly what they refer to.

If I asked you to translate the word "Torah" for someone who wasn't Jewish, you might say it's the Bible, or possibly the Old Testament. That's actually not correct.

The Hebrew Bible is made up of three distinct sections: Torah, Prophets, and Writings. As I mentioned in the last chapter, you are probably somewhat familiar with the Torah and many of the stories and characters that appear there. Most likely, you don't know as much about the other parts.

In Hebrew, the word for Bible is *Tanakh*. The word *Tanakh* is in fact an acronym in Hebrew, meaning that each letter stands for a separate word. In this case, that would be:

Torah   (Teachings, or just translated as Torah)
Nevi'im   (Prophets)
Ketuvim   (Writings)

If you read down the first sounds of the Hebrew words, you get the acronym **TaNaKh**, or (easier to read) *Tanakh*.

You'll notice that the Torah is only one part of the Bible, or *Tanakh*. Actually, it's the smallest part, made up of only five books—the Five Books of Moses, which are Genesis, Exodus, Leviticus, Numbers, and Deuteronomy. In every shul, there's an ark on the *bimah* which holds a number of

Torah scrolls. Each scroll only consists of these five books put together. The rest of the *Tanakh* is written down somewhere else.

Next comes the *Nevi'im* or Prophets section. Your haftarah is an excerpt from one of the books in this section. It describes events that happened long after the episodes in the Torah. Every Torah portion throughout the year is linked with one haftarah from Prophets because of some connection—it may be a similar theme, event, holiday, or character. An interesting challenge is to read through your Torah portion in English, and then your haftarah, and see if you can figure out what the rabbis of old had in mind when they put the two together. Sometimes it's really obvious, and other times the connection is pretty subtle.

Finally, the *Ketuvim* or Writings section is one that you won't have to worry about too much for your bar mitzvah. It contains things like the Psalms, which are recited a lot during services, as well as books for other holidays, like the Scroll of Esther for Purim.

Instead of a little booklet for your haftarah, you might just get a photocopy of the text, or perhaps a folder with the sheets inside. No matter what you get, it'll have everything inside that you'll need.

In some synagogues, you'll start with a Torah reading instead. Just like a haftarah, the Torah is read using special tropes which you'll spend a lot of time learning. Whether you read the Torah, chant a haftarah, or both will simply depend on what your temple usually expects from their b'nei mitzvah students.

In addition to the haftarah and Torah, the other major piece of preparation will revolve around the service and the prayers that you'll be leading. In some temples, each student receives their own *Siddur* at some point, maybe upon finishing a certain grade. You may be asked to bring this *Siddur* to lessons and use it throughout your training. In other cases, your tutor will give you another *Siddur* to use, or a folder with the service photocopied inside.

Why use a folder or booklet instead of just learning out of the regular *Siddur*?

Throughout your lessons, you or your teacher will want to make lots of marks and directions in the book. Since it's not really practical to take a *Siddur* and mark it all up, it makes a lot of sense, at least in the beginning, not

INSIDER'S TIP!

DON'T DOODLE on your folders!
 I know, it sounds really silly. But many students I see
will decorate their folders with squiggles or names or who ♥'s who, or all
the other things that thirteen-year-old kids do to their school notebooks.
Remember that eventually you might be using these folders during your
bar mitzvah service. While you're standing there, all decked out in your
fancy suit or dress, standing in front of the whole congregation, do you
really want to be holding a folder covered with the names of rock groups
and kids who have crushes on each other?

to use the actual pages of the *Siddur*. It's possible that by the time you finish lessons and prepare for the actual bar mitzvah service, your cantor will have you use a *Siddur* just like everyone else in the congregation.

You may also get a recording of some kind of your services and your haftarah or Torah portion. This is the one area where you can tell the difference between old cantors and young cantors. (Hint: If your cantor tells you he learned his haftarah using a record or reel-to-reel tape, he's OLD.)

As technology has evolved, so have the methods by which cantors have been making recordings for their students. I'll spare you the history of sound recordings, but I will point out that up until not that long ago, it was very common for students to get cassette tapes to play at home. (Please just play along and tell me you know what a cassette tape is, even if you've never actually seen one.) I realized that it was time to move on when I tried to place a large order for blank cassettes and the supplier told me they didn't make them anymore.

So then came CDs, which was a lot easier for everyone, because unlike a cassette tape, it became possible to record separate tracks and then just go to the part you wanted to hear. That evolved into mp3 technology, so that you could take the CD and burn it right onto your computer or iPod or other mp3 player, and listen to it that way. It's fun to figure out new ways to make preparation easier. I consider myself pretty tech-savvy, and yet I often learn new things from my students in this area.

JUST FOR PARENTS

C D OR NOT CD—that is the question!
I think that this particular question has been batted
around since Moses got the Ten Commandments from God on Mount Sinai
and asked if God could just record them for the Israelites rather than make
them remember them.

There are two schools of thought on the use of recordings for b'nei
mitzvah students, and each one has merit. Some cantors will not make a
CD or other recording for students, so that the students are required to
learn the trope melodies completely and apply them to the words (more
on that in chapter 3). They believe that if given a recording, students will
simply memorize everything and not really learn how to do it on their own.
This emphasizes the fact that we're teaching students a life-long skill, not
just how to get through one service.

While I definitely agree with that idea, I do regularly hand out CDs to
my students. When I give them a section of haftarah to work on at home,
that's like having problems to solve for homework. The recording becomes
the "answer key." They can check what they're singing and make sure that
they're learning it correctly.

What if your cantor or teacher is a "non-CD" type and you really want
your child to have one? It's always worth a conversation to get a sense of
your teacher's thinking, and see how your son or daughter is progressing.
You may be surprised at how well they can get along without one.

The Lessons

Here we go. This is really the meat of the whole thing, isn't it? Almost every
week for some number of months before your bar mitzvah, you'll have a
lesson. What will they be like?

This really depends on you, and not on the cantor, rabbi, or other tutor
who will be sitting with you. Probably you'll spend some time reviewing
recent material you were supposed to learn, and then a portion of the lesson
will be spent looking at some new stuff. You might also spend some time
discussing the meaning of certain prayers or customs.

My favorite part of lessons is when we can actually take our eyes out of the book and have a conversation. I love to find out where my students are going on vacation, or what their favorite subjects are in school, or other things going on in their lives. I can tell you that this enjoyable kind of chatting is a lot more likely to happen with students who are making good, steady progress and are taking things seriously.

JUST FOR PARENTS

YOU MIGHT be given the choice to sit in on your child's lessons. And even if this is something that you're not invited to do, you always do have the right to be in the cantor's or rabbi's office while your son or daughter is having a lesson. Some of my colleagues will insist that a parent be present during each lesson. Presumably this is so Mom or Dad is also aware of whatever assignment is given and can keep better track of the weekly progress. If you attend, there won't be any surprises down the road, and less chance for any kind of miscommunication.

Sadly, sometimes a cantor will want an adult guardian in the room to avoid any accusation or even appearance of impropriety. I think all teachers today think twice about being in a room alone with a student. That's just an unfortunate reality. Still, I can easily solve that by just making sure my office door is open.

Some parents are just fascinated by the material! Perhaps they never had the chance to learn this subject matter themselves (often the case with mothers) and would love to listen and be educated alongside their kid. That's a pretty nice reason to be present for the lessons.

Still, I think it's the wrong choice.

This is your child's experience, education, and yes, burden. When you sit there, you are making yourself responsible for knowing what she has to practice and how she's progressing. If your daughter doesn't understand something, you will be tempted to ask and get involved. And you will start making excuses for why it was really hard for her to find practicing time this past week ("Well, we had a new cleaning woman who ended up moving all of her folders, and we spent three days looking for them . . .").

Sometimes you're so interested in what's being discussed that you start asking your own questions. There's nothing better than having a member of the congregation want to learn more about the prayers and customs, but this is your child's time, and no matter how good and valuable your question, you're taking away from that. You might look into a better venue for that kind of learning, like an adult education course offered by the synagogue.

Also, this is a great opportunity for your child to establish a relationship with the cantor or rabbi, based on the interaction between the two of them. If you're always present in the room, that won't happen, and your child will miss out.

That's not to say we teachers don't want your involvement! The most successful bar mitzvah kids are the ones whose parents are aware of what they're learning and how they're doing. You should always feel free to call or ask in person, and yes, even to drop in for a few minutes during a lesson. There's certainly nothing wrong with that. I would just advise against always being there.

The Practicing

I know, you were hoping that I forgot about the whole practicing thing. I mean, it all started to sound like so much fun—you have mp3s, and doodling on folders, and chats about vacation destinations with the cantor—who thought there'd be any work to do?

It doesn't have to be a lot of work.

The more you do, the less you have to do.

I can't believe I just wrote that. I sound like one of those Zen masters in a martial arts movie. But there's a lot of wisdom contained in that really strange sentence.

Picture yourself on the day of your bar mitzvah. It *will* happen. You *will* be standing up there and have to sing all the Hebrew words in front of everyone. No one *doesn't* get there.

You do have a couple choices, though, about the road that will take you there, so let's look at both paths.

The First Path

You can avoid putting in a lot of effort for a long time, and go through your lessons, but not really sound so great. But a few weeks before your bar mitzvah, it will really hit you that you're not in good shape. So you'll get very stressed, probably lose some sleep over it, and basically panic.

You won't be alone, because your parents will become involved. Remember, they're the ones who probably have been nagging you for the past six months to practice more, so they want to express a combination of "I told you so" and "Now what are you going to do?" There may be some yelling, grounding, and probably crying.

And when that's over with, you will, in all probability, end up cramming and studying and practicing, and do all the stuff that you should have been doing in the first place. It could be a really rough two or three weeks. But standing up there on the day of your bar mitzvah, no one will know any of that because you'll sound just fine.

Or . . . rewind. Let's try that whole thing again.

The Second Path

You can practice, I don't know, maybe ten or fifteen minutes a day.

You decide to be organized about it, realizing that you don't *really* want to practice, but you have to. You notice that you have homework from school pretty much every day, and you're not particularly crazy about doing that either. So you figure that since you have to do the homework, and you're already in "work mode," then you might as well tack on another ten or so minutes and just do some practicing.

So, reluctantly, you drag out your folders or books, and pop the CD into your laptop (I couldn't have written any of that ten years ago), and start singing. You don't really know what you're doing yet, but the most important thing is that you're doing *something*. You sing along with the cantor's voice on the CD.

After about a week of this, a very funny thing begins to happen. You begin to realize that you already know a few of the paragraphs well enough to sing along strongly. In fact, for some of it, you don't even need the CD playing. When you finish your homework and begin your dreaded ten minutes of practicing, it's really not so dreaded anymore. Plus, you start to spend a little more than ten minutes, and you didn't even notice. Who's looking at the clock when you actually know this stuff?

Another thing. At your next lesson or two, your cantor notices that the small amount of material she gave you to practice sounds pretty good. And now you feel good that she noticed. So she assigns you a little more to work on, which suddenly doesn't feel like such a big deal.

Over the course of weeks and months, you slowly and easily learn each page and every melody, and there you are, same as at the end of the First Path, standing up there doing a nice job in front of everyone. You ended up practicing more, but expending much less effort to get there. You did more, so you could do less!

(A quick and unfortunate Third Path: You never really practice, either now or later, and just don't sound very good. A lot of the Hebrew is butchered and you sound hesitant and unsure of yourself, and somehow muddle through. Even though an occasional child takes this path, I wonder why.)

How Should You Practice?

This is a really good question. Do you try to remember all the tunes that the cantor threw at you? Should you concentrate on just reading the Hebrew first? How much time should you sing along with the CD versus attempting to get through it solo? Is it worth tackling the new stuff or is it better to go through the older, more familiar material?

There isn't really one good answer, and a lot will depend on you and how you learn. Some kids are auditory learners—they hear something and do a really good job at repeating it. Other kids are visual—they need to see it, figure it out, and decode it, and then they'll have a good understanding. Teachers spend years in school and then on the job knowing that no two students really learn the same way. I would recommend that you try various strategies until you find something that makes you comfortable.

For instance, if you're working on either the Torah reading or the haftarah, you will have to deal with a combination of unfamiliar Hebrew words along with a fairly complicated system of tunes attached to those words (the tropes). You may decide to first read through the text a bunch of times so you at least know the Hebrew a little better. Alternately, you could pop the CD in and sing along with the words and melody until you started memorizing it. You could even ignore the words altogether and just figure out how the melody goes.

Each of those methods is perfectly OK, but you'll probably discover that you are most successful using one way more than the others, depending on how your brain works. Remember from my Parable of the Two Paths that the most important thing is to just practice, even if you don't think you're making much headway.

I personally would recommend that you spend as much time as possible using the words and music together as a team. Think about how you learn a song that you like from the radio. You probably don't look up the lyrics, memorize them, and then listen to the melody and put the words to that song. Rather, you sing along with the radio or your iPod repeatedly until you have the song and all the words down. The lyrics don't mean a lot to you without the music that goes with them. I find learning a haftarah or page out of the *Siddur* to be the same way.

Do you disagree? Fantastic—prove me wrong! Practice any way that you think is effective for you. I'm no expert on how you learn; you are.

INSIDER'S TIP!

EVERY **NOW** and then a student comes along who is very talented musically. She has a beautiful voice, sings in the choir, and plays three instruments. As we're practicing together, she sings with me and it's a breath of fresh air. When I hear her sing some of the prayers, it sounds wonderful.

You would think that a student like this has a tremendous advantage because the music part seems to be all set. Because she can sing anything, she'll really only need to worry about the reading aspect.

It's ironic that I often find these talented musicians have a tougher time than most "average" kids. I believe it's because their musical ear is so discerning it's hard for them to get any note wrong and just go on. Their brains are telling them that it's wrong unless they get every single tune exactly a certain way—because it just doesn't sound correct. Another student who sounds just fine but isn't as musical will just sing and not worry about perfect accuracy (and will sound normal and pleasant to everyone else).

Appearances can be deceiving. When you hear a bar mitzvah kid singing beautifully from the *bimah*, his road to get there might have been even more challenging than average.

The Bottom Line

Since your bar mitzvah is supposed to be when you start the long process of thinking about how you want to observe Judaism, let it also be how you begin to treat challenges and obstacles in your life. Months of preparation and practicing, culminating with you singing confidently in front of your family and friends—this is how you want to look back and remember that you were able to tackle what seemed unthinkably impossible just a short time before.

May I sound all Zen one more time? This is more about the journey than the destination. The real challenge is how you approach this process, and the decisions that you make along the way about practicing and preparing. It's something that your parents can't do for you, even if they nag you to practice. The so-called rite of passage isn't at all about standing up on the *bimah* in fancy, uncomfortable clothes and chanting some tunes but rather about how you face down your first adult-sized challenge.

If you can do it then, you can do it again. And again.

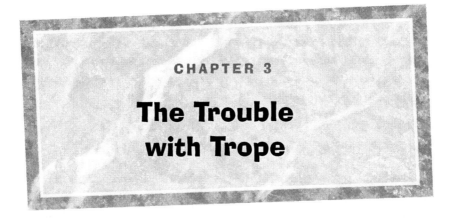

CHAPTER 3

The Trouble with Trope

I'**S LIKELY** that you will be introduced to trope on your very first bar mitzvah lesson. Never has one concept caused so much suffering in the hearts and minds of Jewish thirteen-year-olds throughout history. And that's so unnecessary; learning the trope symbols and melodies is actually fairly simple.

What Is Trope?

Before we do anything, look at any funny shapes, or figure out any tunes, let's go over what the actual word "trope" refers to. You may be surprised to learn that there's nothing particularly Jewish about the word; it can mean different things depending on whether you're talking about music, literature, languages, and of course, the Jewish Bible, or *Tanakh*. I know you don't care about any of those other definitions, but somewhere down the road you may be sitting in some advanced literary analysis class and your professor will start to discuss a recurring trope present in a work you're reading. I wouldn't want you to raise your hand and say, "I know all about this; I had bar mitzvah lessons!"

For our purposes, you should know that tropes tell us the way to sing different sections of the Bible.

During your bar mitzvah, you are likely going to sing from two differ-ent places in the Bible. You might learn a Torah reading, which is an excerpt from the Torah, and of course your haftarah, which comes from a different, later section of the *Tanakh*—the Prophets. Each of these texts is sung to a distinct melody using trope.

How Does Trope Tell How to Sing Anything?

A while ago, I was an invited guest at a bar mitzvah celebration, and the DJ was entertaining the kids out on the dance floor so the adults could eat their meals while the kids were occupied. Sure enough, the DJ started to play a game called "Coke and Pepsi." I have never been to any bar mitzvah party where Coke and Pepsi isn't played, so I usually don't pay that much attention.

This time, though, I started watching and suddenly had an "Aha!" moment. Luckily I didn't shout it out loud, or everyone would have looked at me pretty strangely over their salads.

For the two or three people left in the country who are unfamiliar with Coke and Pepsi, let me sum up how the game is played. The DJ lines up two rows of kids on either side of the dance floor, facing each other. He then tells everyone that when he says "Coke!" all the kids on *this* side have to run over to their partners on *that* side. When he yells "Pepsi!" the kids on *that* side have to run over to *this* side. Then there are other beverage names he'll call—Mountain Dew, Dr. Pepper, Sprite, and so on—that will mean other specific actions that the kids have to perform, like freezing, or kneel-ing down, and other silly stuff. Each time he calls something, the last pair of teammates to do the required action is out.

While I was watching the kids play, I realized that this is how trope works! Trope is Coke and Pepsi for your haftarah and Torah reading.

What if, instead of the DJ explaining what his different beverage names meant, he told everyone that he was going to give them ten complicated actions to do which they'd have to memorize. Well, first, the game wouldn't be much fun, and second, kids would find it pretty hard to memorize all those things to do.

Luckily, the DJ can accomplish the same thing by making each beverage name *stand for* a different action. He can just say "Coke!" and in a very easy

and effortless way, he has communicated to an entire room full of scream-
ing kids that he would like everyone on his left to run as quickly as possible
over to everyone on his right. Similarly, all of his other words quickly and
efficiently tell the kids to do somewhat complicated actions.

Put another way, the beverage names are code.

So is trope.

I could give you three pages of strange Hebrew and tell you to learn and
memorize every single tune. That's theoretically possible, but pretty difficult
and miserable to do. Instead, let's learn a bunch of trope symbols. These
symbols will be like a code—if you just memorize them (the same as you
had to memorize a few words in Coke and Pepsi), then you'll be able to sing
as much haftarah or Torah as you want, whenever you want.

Trope is the secret code for how to sing any haftarah or Torah reading.
During your lessons, you'll easily learn how to crack the code. Tropes are
symbols—shapes or lines or curvy things—that appear either over or under
every single word in the Bible. In fact, sometimes they're just referred to as
trope symbols. Each symbol has two things: a name and a melody.

We can look at specific trope symbols, but the one thing that we'll find
it hard to do right now is to learn how to sing anything. There's no CD that
accompanies this book, and it would be really tiring for me to appear in all
of your homes and sing for you. Plus, there are a lot of minor differences in
how different people have learned trope. Even if I could sing for you right
now, it might be just slightly different than the way your cantor would teach
you, and then you'd get confused.

Let's just get a really good feel for what trope looks like and how it works.

Meet the Tropes!

There are well over twenty different trope symbols, and I'm not going to
include all of them. Instead, I'll point out a few common ones that you're
likely to see all the time.

Some tropes appear under the word, and others are placed over the word,
and that will never change for any trope symbol. I'll give you the name of
the trope along with its symbol. Here are some of the most common trope
combinations; you'll come across these very often and probably learn them
at your first lesson.

mahpach	אַ	mercha	אַ
pashta	אַ	tipcha	אַ
munach	אַ	munach	אַ
katon	אַ	etnachta	אַ

The Hebrew letter is where you would see a Hebrew word, so you can see if a certain trope is over or under the word. You'll also notice that the trope names are quite strange sounding! They are in fact Aramaic words, not Hebrew.

Together with your cantor, you'll learn a little two- or three-note melody for each of those tropes. Then, when you look at your Torah reading or haftarah, you'll see that every word has a trope of its own, and because the tropes that I just showed you are so common, you'll see those in many places. You simply take the little melody that you learned and sing the Hebrew word to that same tune. The trope symbol acts as a code for how to sing the word.

INSIDER'S TIP!

ARAMAIC WAS a language that was commonly spoken a couple thousand years ago, much like English is today. Hebrew used to be reserved only for holy texts, like the Torah and prayers, so all day-to-day communication would be in Aramaic. The two languages are related to each other in that they use the same alphabet and share a lot of the same roots that make up each language's vocabulary, sort of like English and Spanish.

Some of the prayers that we still recite today are actually in Aramaic—because these prayers used to be so popular and recited so often even by people who didn't know Hebrew they have survived in their original form. Well-known examples are the Mourners' Kaddish and the *Kol Nidrei* prayer that's recited every year on Yom Kippur.

The tropes also go so far back that their names are Aramaic. Each name has a meaning—usually a descriptive word to help identify the trope symbol.

Putting It Together

I know, I make it sound incredibly effortless. If in fact it were just that easy, you wouldn't need months of bar mitzvah lessons and seemingly endless practicing. The idea itself *is* pretty easy: Learn a trope's simple tune, find a Hebrew word that has that trope symbol, and sing the word to that tune.

The difficulty arises because unless you're a champion Hebrew reader, it will take a little bit of decoding on your part to read the word. Then your brain has to remember those couple notes that you learned, and then you have to put the two things together. Then you have to do the same thing for the next word, all the while keeping what you just did in mind so you don't forget that. Obviously, practicing will make this a lot easier for you.

There are different strategies that you can use. You could take a trope that you're learning and try to find it as many times as you can on a page. Then sing every word on that page. This is helpful because you're doing two important things: (1) you're getting good at finding and identifying a certain trope symbol and (2) you're reinforcing that tune in your head. I bet if you did this, by the time you got to the bottom of the page, you'd be really good at that one trope.

I find that students end up just trying to memorize the whole thing. After all, why not? You have all the words, and probably received a CD or other type of recording of the whole haftarah or Torah reading. You can simply listen, sing along, and eventually just learn it well enough to sing it by yourself.

That might work. But doing it that way is fraught with risks. First, if you think you have the whole thing committed to memory, and somewhere in the middle you blank out and forget how a word gets sung, what are you going to do? You have no way to get back on the tune.

Second, and really more important, you're not really accomplishing what we had in mind for your bar mitzvah lessons. Remember that the tropes are a way to sing *any* Torah reading or haftarah. If you simply memorize a few pages of haftarah, for instance, and sing it flawlessly at your bar mitzvah, what you've really demonstrated is that you're a talented parrot. You took a recording, memorized it, and sang it right back. This is why some cantors don't routinely hand out CDs to the b'nei mitzvah students.

But if you make the effort to learn a relatively small number of tropes, you now possess the tools to sing a haftarah or Torah reading any week, not just at your bar mitzvah service.

Think about it like this: The first way says that your service is the end of all your training. The second way shows that your participation is just beginning.

Another strategy for practicing has to do with looking at trope phrases.

Grammar Fun

Yup, I did it. I used the g-word. I told you before that I love grammar. Trope doesn't only tell us how to sing the word, but also a ton more information. That's why it's so important.

Trope symbols are sometimes called "accents," and this makes perfect sense, since in addition to musical information, trope symbols actually tell us exactly how to accent the word.

I'll show you. Say this sentence out loud:

I think cantors are incredibly cool.

(I can't believe how easy it was for me to get you to say that.)

Now let's pretend that someone can read English pretty well but didn't understand a word. If he were just figuring out the words one after the other, it might sound something like this:

I think. canTORS are. increDIBly. cool.

See how our imaginary reader is just sounding out words, doing the best he can? In fact, if you read this second version out loud, it sounds a lot like a computer reading, doesn't it? What if there was a way to tell the reader exactly how to accent longer words?

Maybe we could write things the way you see it in a dictionary.

I think can'-tors are in-cre'-dib-ly cool.

See what I did there? I put in accent marks next to certain parts of the word. That told a reader who was unfamiliar with the words precisely how to pronounce them. We have exactly the same thing in Hebrew—but instead of using a little apostrophe for an accent, we have tropes.

The tropes aren't just thrown on a Hebrew word anywhere. They're carefully placed either under or over exactly that part of the Hebrew word that gets accented. Let's look at an actual Hebrew word, with a trope, and see how that works. It's fine if you don't read Hebrew; I'll tell you how to pronounce it.

וְאָהַבְתָּ

You may recognize this word. It comes from the Book of Deuteronomy, and begins a well-known paragraph that is recited after we sing the *Shema*. If you are able to read Hebrew, go ahead and try reading it out loud right now.

I can't prove it, but I'm guessing that you read it wrong. I bet this is what you said:

ve-ah-HAV-ta

Yup, 'fess up. I know you did.
In fact, the proper way to say this word is as follows:

ve-AH-hav-TA

Two questions come to mind: How do we know this? And why do we care?

First, we look back at the Hebrew word and we see some tropes there. If you're a beginning Hebrew reader, it's easy to confuse the vowels with tropes, but eventually you'll be able to distinguish them. There are actually two tropes present. One is *under* the second letter and the other is *over* the final letter.

In addition to telling us how to sing this word, which we would know after we spent some time learning how to sing those tropes, these symbols tell us how to *read* the word as well. We should accent the word exactly on the places where the tropes are. So the second letter, which makes the AH sound, and the last letter, which makes the TA sound, are the places to accent.

This becomes really important for a couple reasons. First, if you accent each word properly, you'll sound great! Most students learn how to read Hebrew pretty well, but rarely learn what the words mean. That's just the way things are for most Jewish kids and adults. But if you read a text through, properly accenting and phrasing words, you'll sound like a Hebrew expert.

Also, sometimes just moving one little accent completely changes the meaning of the word! I picked this word on purpose because it fits this category. The Hebrew word that I showed you means "you shall love." It's a specific biblical form that comes up countless times, where they take a word in past tense, stick a certain letter in front of it, and make it a future tense. Therefore, you can't tell the difference between the words meaning "you shall love" and "you loved." Except for the accent.

Ve-ah-HAV-ta (the wrong way that everyone says) means "you loved."

Ve-AH-hav-TA means "you shall love."

You don't need to be a Hebrew scholar or linguistic expert to know any of this. Just use the tropes as accents and all the work will instantly be done for you.

The Punctuation Game

The Hebrew Bible was originally passed down orally from one generation to the next. It wasn't written down; there were certainly no books at that time, and it was uncommon for texts to be handwritten on parchment or papyrus. Instead, traditions were carefully preserved by telling and re-telling information over the course of many years.

So when the Torah was first put down in writing, there wasn't just one accepted way of writing the text. Sure, they had most of the words, but they were originally written down without any vowels. In English, where vowels are part of the written language, our words would turn into gibberish without them. Thngs wld lk lk ths.

But Hebrew letters are all consonants, so you can write perfectly well without vowels. Most modern Hebrew, like in books and newspapers, is written without vowels. Fluent readers know the language well enough that they know how to pronounce each word. In the prayer book, however, all the vowels are provided, as they are when learning Torah and your haftarah.

In addition to the original text of the Torah having vowels, the trope symbols were also added at a later time. We've learned so far that tropes tell us how to sing the words, as well as how to place proper accents. But another very important function of the tropes is to phrase and punctuate every sentence. A simple way to understand this is to know that some tropes essentially work as commas. They divide the sentence into shorter phrases.

Just like I told you that a simple accent can change the whole meaning of a word, so too can the placement of punctuation. Consider the following sentence, written without a key piece of punctuation:

Please go to the post office and get me thirty two cent stamps.

Let me ask you: How many stamps are you going to get? How much money should I give you?

For want of a simple hyphen, the entire sentence could mean two separate things.

Option 1: Please go to the post office and get me thirty two-cent stamps. You'll need sixty cents and will walk out of there with thirty stamps.

Option 2: Please go to the post office and get me thirty-two cent stamps. I guess I'm leaving it up to you how many to get. I hope I gave you enough money.

Here's another amusing example:

Woman without her man is nothing.

Whoa! When did I turn into such a male chauvinist? Do I really think that a woman without a man is nothing? Of course not—I would punctuate that sentence like this:

Woman—without her, man is nothing.

Turned that one right around, didn't I? I added a strategically placed dash and comma and completely flipped the meaning around.

Here's one of my favorites:

Let's eat Bill.

I bet when you bought this book you didn't think there'd be any mention of cannibalism, did you?

The life-saving power of one simple comma:

Let's eat, Bill.

That made a pretty big difference, didn't it? (Bill sure thinks so.)

Tropes do the same thing by dividing every single sentence into clauses and phrases just like I did with my English examples. For you, this becomes as important as putting the right accents on the words. It makes you sound really good when you're chanting or singing your haftarah or Torah reading.

Like we did before, let's pretend that you can read English just fine but have no idea what the words mean. Read the following sentence:

It began to rain so before I left the house I called up to my mother to get my umbrella the one I left in my closet.

If you read it just like that, most people could figure out what you were trying to say, but it wouldn't really sound like English. However, if I put some punctuation in there for you, even if you didn't understand one word of what you were reading, you would sound like a native English speaker.

It began to rain, so before I left the house, I called up to my mother to get my umbrella—the one I left in my closet.

We haven't changed the meaning of the sentence, but it just sounds so much better. You can easily accomplish the same thing when you pay attention to certain tropes. They become the commas and other punctuation. When you start learning tropes in your lessons, your cantor can point out a few tropes that help you divide up the sentence, which you can very easily remember.

Where Did It All Come From?

Tropes were probably the very first public address system. Back in the days before electricity and microphones and amplifiers, people still had to give speeches before large crowds, and the idea was to get as many people as possible to be able to hear.

INSIDER'S TIP!

HEBREW SCHOOL teachers usually do a fantastic job of teaching kids how to read Hebrew over the years. The result is that by the time students walk into bar mitzvah lessons, their reading is usually at a decent enough level that we can dive right into the material and start learning tunes and tropes.

One thing that I don't think teachers spend enough time on is phrasing and punctuation. Open up any *Siddur* and you'll see that the text is written just like English, with commas, dashes, and periods. Yet most kids get in the habit of simply ignoring these and read the words, one after the other. Because they don't understand the actual words, they concentrate on only the pronunciation of individual words rather than putting the whole thing together.

Don't just read words. Read sentences. Get in the habit of paying attention to punctuation in Hebrew and you'll not only read accurately, but what you're saying will actually *mean* something.

In our modern services every week, we read from the Torah and the congregation listens or follows along. Back in ancient times, though, the Torah was read in public not in the synagogue, because those didn't really exist yet, but rather in the public square where people would gather. This would take place on Mondays and Thursdays, the common market days when the most number of people could be found in one location. Today we remember that by also reading the Torah in our morning weekday services on Monday and Thursday.

The reader would have to enunciate very well and have his voice heard by as many people as possible. To imagine how this is related to certain tropes, let's look at another English sentence (maybe one that you would like to hear in temple).

I am very happy to announce that there will be a big lunch following services today.

Now I want you to get in character a bit, and imagine standing on a podium outside, addressing a huge crowd of people. Try reading it slowly, loudly, and emphasizing some words and pausing a bit after others, so that you really deliver the meaning of the sentence. It works even better if you put on an English accent. You might read it something like this:

I am very HAPPY to ANNOUNCE that there will be a BIG LUNCH following SERVICES today.

Did you see how your voice naturally rose while saying some words (usually the ones that I capitalized), and fell off during others. Additionally, you probably paused a bit between certain thoughts. If you ever have to do any public speaking in school, you might want to try this technique (but you should probably drop the English accent).

Tropes came about as a way to reflect the natural rise and fall of the voice when delivering a message. We have a few common tropes that directly relate to these changes in pitch. Here are just a couple of examples, and ones that you will learn very early on and see all the time.

These first two are read from right to left (like in Hebrew). The first trope, *kadma*, is just a little intro in the main idea, *mahpach*. It's the way you would begin to read many sentences.

mahpach   kadma

אֲ   אֱ

This next trope, *pashta*, is usually sung higher. That's one of those rising words we looked at before. The *pashta* might emphasize an important word.

pashta

אֱ

By the way, extra credit for you if you looked carefully and couldn't tell the difference between the little curvy symbol for kadma and pashta. You're not going crazy; they are in fact the same shape. There are easy and simple ways to tell the difference that you'll see once you start learning trope.

Finally, another one of the tropes we looked at earlier,

etnachta

אֱ

usually appears once in every sentence and works like a big comma. It's when you take a pause in the sentence.

Certainly, I wouldn't expect you to become an expert on any of this just by reading this section. During your lessons, you'll begin to learn the trope symbols and how they are sung. Many of them, like the ones I've shown you here, are extremely common and are repeated countless times. Others come up less frequently, but you won't have any trouble figuring them out. Hopefully, when you really get familiar with tropes in your lessons, you'll use them to not only sing the words but also to accent and phrase the sentences beautifully as well.

Now Let's Read Some Torah

I've been saving the hard part for last. OK, not too hard, just a bit different.

If you look at a page of haftarah and a page taken from the Torah, they will look exactly the same. You have Hebrew text with our now-familiar tropes under or over every word. And you know that every trope has its own little melody attached to it.

Unfortunately, that little melody will be different depending on whether you're singing Torah or haftarah. That's right, the tunes that you've spent so long singing with your haftarah will change for the Torah.

However, fear not. Frequently the changes in melody are pretty minor. Often, if you learned that a certain trope for haftarah starts low and goes high, for instance, chances are very good that the same trope for Torah does

INSIDER'S TIP!

IT'S NOT ETCHED in stone that a student learns haftarah first and then moves to a Torah reading. In fact, in some synagogues, the opposite is true.

In most Conservative shuls, it's traditional to begin with the haftarah. In many Reform temples, students may be given the Torah reading first, and then required to learn some of that week's haftarah. As with a lot of things that I discuss, it all depends on your particular synagogue and its policies. There's no one absolute way to do things.

basically the same thing, but maybe just changes a little bit. Some tropes are actually sung the same way for both haftarah and Torah, whereas others are considerably different. The bottom line is that once you have put some time and effort into learning one system of melodies for tropes, your brain is already used to decoding those symbols, and you'll put in *much* less time learning new ones.

There's yet another significant difference between reading your haftarah and doing a Torah reading. When you chant your haftarah at your bar mitzvah, you will almost certainly be reading from whatever booklet or folder your cantor or teacher prepared for you. It will be easy to read, and have whatever little markings or arrows or notes that you wrote in to remind you of different things you wanted to remember.

Torah reading, though . . . well, that's different. Traditionally, one reads Torah right out of the Torah scroll. Your shul probably has a good number of Torah scrolls in the ark in the sanctuary. During the service, one of the Torah scrolls is taken out of the ark and opened up, and the person who is doing the Torah reading, whether it's the cantor, rabbi, a member of the congregation, or you, must read it directly out of the scroll. It's the only time you won't be able to use your own book or folder.

Further complicating matters is the fact that the Torah scroll is written in a fancy calligraphy, and . . . wait for it . . . has no vowels, trope symbols, or punctuation of any kind. Just the words.

Here is a verse of Torah from Deuteronomy. It's the complete sentence after the one word that I showed you several pages ago.

וְאָהַבְתָּ אֵת יְהֹוָה אֱלֹהֶיךָ בְּכָל־לְבָבְךָ וּבְכָל־נַפְשְׁךָ וּבְכָל־מְאֹדֶךָ׃

(And you shall love the Lord your God with all your heart and all your soul and all your might.)

Even if you can't read it very well, you may notice that the words have vowels and trope symbols, as well as the colon at the end, which is the same as a period. So if you get good at all the things I've pointed out to you so far, you'll be able to sing this sentence, accent every word correctly, make your voice go up or pause when appropriate, and stop when you come to the end.

However, if you find this exact same sentence in the actual Torah scroll, it's not going to look like that. Here's what you'll see instead:

ואהבת את יהוה אלהיך בכל לבבך ובכל נפשך ובכל מאדך

Poof—all your vowels and tropes disappeared. So how in the world are you supposed to know how to read and sing that? The answer: Don't worry!

You will spend as much time as you need learning the words and tropes from a book or folder that has all the markings in it. It's only when you're good at it and know the material well that you'll start trying to read it from the actual Torah scroll. At that point, you'll be amazed at how easy it will be for you.

Another advantage you have is that the length of any Torah reading that you'll be doing may be much, much shorter than the haftarah. Typically, you'll be assigned a short paragraph to prepare. You can do more than that, depending on your shul, but it won't be a lot to learn.

INSIDER'S TIP!

YOU'VE ALREADY learned about two different ways that the tropes are sung—one way for the haftarah and another for Torah. In fact, there are six distinct musical systems for the tropes!

Each of these parts of the Bible is sung differently using the same tropes:

1. Books of the Prophets (every haftarah comes from here)
2. Torah (first Five Books of Moses)
3. Torah when read on Rosh Hashanah and Yom Kippur (yes, a special tune just for those holidays)
4. The Scroll of Esther, which is read on the holiday of Purim
5. The Book of Lamentations, a very sad book that we read on Tisha B'av, a day in the Jewish calendar which recalls a series of terrible disasters that befell the Jewish people
6. The Books of Ruth (read on Shavuot), Ecclesiastes (read on Sukkot), and Song of Songs (read on Passover)

To make it even more fun, there are several places where you actually switch tunes in the middle! For instance, a person who is singing the Scroll of Esther needs to switch *mid-sentence* into the tune for Lamentations, and then back again. It can certainly become challenging. Luckily, for now you don't have to learn anything more than the Torah and haftarah trope.

Finally, every synagogue is different. In most Conservative shuls, the Torah reader is required to read right out of the scroll, like I've just described. In other temples, it may be permissible to read out of a *Chumash* (special book which contains the Torah readings and haftarot), or a sheet which someone photocopied for you. You'll find out the requirements of your particular temple as you go through lessons.

There is one more thing to keep in mind as you prepare to tackle Torah reading. In my experience, this is the number one skill that parents wish they had and are always sorry they never learned. You're actually lucky to be learning this!

The Bottom Line

Tropes are the not-so-secret code to learn your haftarah or Torah reading. Contained within every one of those funny looking little lines or curvy shapes is a vast amount of information which includes how to sing each word, where to place the accents, and how to punctuate the complete text. That's a pretty efficient use of a symbol, don't you think?

Once you break the code, you will be able to sing any haftarah or Torah reading, not just the one you're spending all the time on right now.

CHAPTER 4

Everything You Ever Wanted to Know about the Jewish Calendar

BACK IN chapter 1, I told you that just by virtue of reaching your thirteenth birthday you become bar mitzvah. But you may remember that I added one little detail—I said the thirteenth birthday *according to the Jewish calendar.*

What does that mean? Is it something much different?

When I teach this subject to kids and adults, this is always the point when I ask who's good at math. A few hands creep up. Who is interested in astronomy? Maybe a few more hands get raised. Of course, you don't need to be a math genius or Carl Sagan to appreciate the design of the Jewish calendar. (I did it again, didn't I? Parents, would you please tell your kids who Carl Sagan was? Thanks.)

So let's start trying to figure out what makes the Jewish calendar so special and how it differs from our own familiar set of dates.

The calendar that we all know and love goes by different names. The fancy term is the Gregorian calendar, also known as the Western calendar and sometimes even the Christian calendar. I'm going to make things as easy as possible and simply call it "the regular calendar."

The regular calendar is a solar calendar. (This brings new meaning to the term "hot date.") All this means is that our calendar is based on the cycle and movement of the sun, which becomes pretty obvious if you think about it. The year is divided into four seasons, which have to do with the way the earth is positioned in relation to the sun. Our regular year lasts 365 days because it takes that long for the earth to revolve all the way around the sun.

Yes, this is when the nerdy kid sitting in the back says, "It actually takes 365¼ days, which is why we have leap years every four years."

True, but for now, we don't care about any of that. In fact, I'm going to do the best I can to keep things very simple and round numbers off whenever I can.

The Jewish calendar is a lunar calendar, which means that unlike the regular calendar, it is based on the moon, not the sun. Try to picture yourself living thousands of years ago, before technology, electricity, or Facebook. Back then, you didn't have a calendar hanging in your kitchen. Rather, you kept track of the passage of time by *observing* things. You kept track of seasons by watching the days get longer and warmer, and then eventually shorter and colder. And of course, each night, it was very easy to look up and see the moon, which if you looked really carefully, changed a little every single night.

It was a perfect way to keep track of time, because the moon itself acted like a little calendar.

Now here's where things get a little tricky. Remember I said before that if we added up all the days it took for the earth to go completely around the sun, we'd get 365. Similarly, if we did the same thing for the moon to go through twelve complete cycles, we would get the number 354.

Therefore, the regular year is 365 days long, and the Jewish (or lunar) year is 354 days long.

That means that the Jewish year is eleven days shorter than the regular year.

INSIDER'S TIP!

DID YOU ever notice that the word "moon" and "month" are so similar? Obviously that's no coincidence; the two words come from the same place. The Jewish calendar is one of a number of ancient calendars that use the moon to keep track of months. The idea that one month equals one cycle of the moon is the cornerstone of every major calendar.

That's a problem. A pretty significant problem. This means that each year that passes, all the Jewish days and holidays are going to occur eleven days earlier. Year after year, eleven days earlier each time.

And this is precisely the spot where I watch eyes glaze over and heads droop. No one ever really gets this part!

So let me try to explain it in a way that I think you'll understand.

Start with the Jewish holiday of Rosh Hashanah, the Jewish New Year. You don't need to know anything at all about this holiday right now other than the fact that it occurs on the first day of the first month of the Jewish calendar—it's the *New Year*. I will tell you that the name of the first Jewish month is called *Tishrei*.

Quiz question #1: What is the Hebrew date of Rosh Hashanah?

Deep breath. You know this! Rosh Hashanah is the first day of the Jewish calendar. Tishrei is the first month of the Jewish calendar. Therefore, yup, you got it, Rosh Hashanah falls on the first day of Tishrei.

1 Tishrei = Rosh Hashanah.

In order to help you understand how the Jewish calendar works alongside the regular calendar, let's think about some average regular year. In this made-up average year, we'll imagine that Rosh Hashanah falls on September 16. That makes sense, right? That certainly seems like a reasonably possible time for Rosh Hashanah to occur.

So in my made-up year,

September 16 = Rosh Hashanah = 1 Tishrei

Great. I hope you're still with me. Now I want you to imagine a long, straight path, made up of large bricks laid out one after the other. You're standing on the first brick, and when you look down, you see etched into the brick the words "September 16."

You take a step onto the next brick, which you imagine takes you to the next date, September 17.

Each brick that you step on is one more date.

Finally, after a nice leisurely walk, you reach the end of the brick path. You've come to the last brick, and you look down and read the words "September 16."

Quiz question #2: How many bricks did you walk on?

Sure, that's easy. You walked on 365 bricks. You just walked your way through the regular calendar, from one day this year to the same day the next year. That took you 365 days, or in our exercise, 365 bricks.

Can you still picture the long brick path? Now imagine there is a second long, straight path, right next to it. There are two brick paths, side by side, and they look the same. But because there are two paths to walk on, you need to grab a friend to help you out.

There you are back on your first brick. Just like before, you look down and see the words "September 16." But your friend looks down at her brick next to you and *that* brick says "Rosh Hashanah, 1 Tishrei" on it.

Right now, you two are standing next to each other, on the same day.

You're September 16 in the regular year, and she's 1 Tishrei in the Jewish year.

Both of you take one step.

Now, you're standing on September 17 and she's on 2 Tishrei.

You and your friend never separate; you're always standing right next to each other on your own brick paths. Every step you take puts you one day later in the regular calendar, and each step she takes represents one day later in the Jewish calendar.

Quiz question #3: Are the two paths the same length?

Think about it. Your path is the regular year, so it is exactly 365 bricks long. Her path is the Jewish year, so it only goes on for 354 bricks. She's going to come to the end of her path while you still have eleven bricks left.

When your friend is standing on her last brick, and you are standing next to her, look down and read the words etched in both of your bricks. Hers will say "Rosh Hashanah, 1 Tishrei" on it, because she came to the end of her path, the Jewish year. She went 354 days from one New Year to the next New Year.

What day are you standing on? Of course, it is *not* September 16, is it? You haven't gotten all the way to the end of your path yet. You are, as we said, eleven bricks short. Therefore, you are standing on a brick that says "September 5."

When your friend was ready to celebrate Rosh Hashanah again, the Jewish New Year, it fell that time on September 5. It came eleven days earlier.

Now you can see where I'm going with this lunar calendar business. Every Jewish date, every Jewish holiday would occur eleven days earlier each year.

In my two imaginary years, Rosh Hashanah occurred on September 16 the first year, and then September 5 the next year, which doesn't really sound like a big deal. It might be a little inconvenient coming so close to the beginning of a school year, but otherwise, it's fine.

Quiz question #4: Ah, but what happens the next year?

That's right, now you can begin to see what I'm trying to show you. Rosh Hashanah will get *another* eleven days earlier. If you grab any calendar from any year, find September 5, and count back eleven days, you'll land on August 25.

That's way too early for Rosh Hashanah. It would never happen. Rosh Hashanah always falls somewhere between Labor Day weekend and maybe the first week of October. Similarly, Chanukah will always come between Thanksgiving weekend (and that's really early for it, isn't it?) and Christmas. Passover is also known as the Festival of Spring, so certainly it must be celebrated at some point from late March through mid-April.

Many of the Jewish holidays are tied to certain points in the Jewish calendar, and except for some minor moving around every year, they have to stay in the same general location. How do we do that, then, if I showed you that things are scheduled to get eleven days earlier every single year?

Dim the lights please, and cue the dramatic music.

Enter . . . the JEWISH LEAP YEAR!

Remember that nerdy kid I mentioned before? He's the one who insisted that the earth actually took 365¼ days to complete the rotation around the sun. Therefore, every four years in the regular calendar, we need to add an extra day, February 29, in order to keep our solar calendar aligned with the solar years.

There are leap years in the Jewish calendar too, but they're completely different. Instead of adding one day every four years, the Jewish calendar

INSIDER'S TIP!

HOW OFTEN do we have a Jewish leap year? It's not as simple as saying "every three years" or something like that. The answer is that over the course of nineteen years, there is a repeating pattern of leap and common (non-leap) years. We add that extra leap month in seven out of the nineteen years.

That makes it a little more complicated and is really more than most people need to know in order to understand how the Jewish calendar works. I just included the information here, tucked away in this Insider's Tip, for you readers who *just can't get enough!*

adds *an entire month* every two or three years. So the Jewish calendar, rather than being purely lunar, is really *lunisolar*, and no, I did not just make that word up. As you can probably guess, it describes a calendar which is based partly on the cycle of the moon, and partly on the rotation of the earth around the sun.

Let me say this again. Every now and then, a whole month is added to the Jewish calendar! Do you know what that means? That's right, better call the brickyard, you've got some paving to do.

Your friend's brick path is about to get longer. You have to add thirty more bricks onto her path (one month of bricks).

Come on, get back up. We don't call this bar mitzvah training for nothing. Go stand at the beginning of your brick path again. Remind me, what's the date etched on your first brick? Right, September 16. Did your friend get up too? She should be standing on her first brick, right next to you, as always. Her first brick also didn't change. It still says "Rosh Hashanah, 1 Tishrei."

Start walking.

I hope your friend is in good shape, because her path just got longer. She has thirty more bricks to cover. She's walking on a "leap" path—a path that gets an extra month of bricks.

When you get to the end of your path, as expected, you will look down and see September 16. In my previous example, your friend had already reached the end of her path. *This time,* though, she's still walking.

Quiz question #5: How many more bricks will your friend have to walk after you're done?

STOP! Don't answer yet!

I know you want to say thirty. You have that number in your head. I told you a million times that there are thirty more bricks in her path, so you think she's going to be walking an extra thirty steps after you're done. In fact, the answer is . . . wait for it . . . nineteen! Your friend will be walking on nineteen more bricks after you stop on September 16.

How? Why? I can hear the sound of books slamming shut and Kindles being powered down all over the country.

In my original brick path example, your friend stopped eleven bricks short of you, didn't she? But we've since added thirty bricks to her path. So she gets to cover those missing eleven bricks plus nineteen more, for a total of thirty extra "leap" bricks.

Your friend's new path now contains 384 bricks. There were the original 354 that we started with, plus the extra thirty that I made her put in while I was taking a break from writing and getting a cup of coffee.

She walks her extra nineteen bricks after you get to stop. Looking down at her last brick, just like before, she sees "Rosh Hashanah, 1 Tishrei." Even though it was longer this time, her brick path always represents one Jewish year, so if she started on Rosh Hashanah, she's going to end on Rosh Hashanah.

She looks back over her shoulder, sees you standing way back at the end of your path (on September 16), and shouts, "Come on! Get over here!"

Well, you're out of bricks on your path, but that's OK. You carefully take nineteen more steps so that you're standing next to her once again. If you hadn't run out of bricks, you would have stepped on nineteen more bricks in order to stand side by side with your friend. Since you ran out back at September 16, you would have added nineteen more days (bricks), and therefore, you would now be standing next to your friend at . . . October 5.

OK, everyone sit down and take a break from all this walking while I sum things up.

Every Jewish holiday will come eleven days earlier each year that passes.

But, if there is a Jewish leap year, then every Jewish holiday will then come nineteen days *later*.

You become bar or bat mitzvah when you have reached your thirteenth birthday according to this Jewish calendar. Put another way, if you started walking on that second brick path when you were born, you would have to complete thirteen trips.

You should know what your birthday is in the Jewish calendar, and there are a couple different ways to find out. First, and probably the easiest, is to simply ask your rabbi or cantor. For instance, I have a book that functions as a two-hundred-year calendar so that I can instantly match up any regular date to its Jewish equivalent.

As an example, I know that I was born on the first day of the Hebrew month of Kislev. (I know the names of the months sound funny; I'll go over all of them a little later.) In order to find my birthday in the Jewish calendar any year, I just go to the date 1 Kislev and find out when it falls. It may be slightly before my real birthday, or a little after.

JUST FOR PARENTS

HANDING OUT the dates for all the b'nei mitzvah in the temple each year is probably the worst job anyone could get. No one is happy; everyone complains.

This will depend a lot on what size temple you belong to, and what their specific policies are. Sometimes there is more than one bar mitzvah going on at the same time, but in different rooms (if it's a big shul). Other times, you may be asked or required to "double up," that is, share a date with another family. Perhaps the date you were assigned is right in the middle of winter and you're nervous about a blizzard on your big day. Finally, what happens if your child's Hebrew birthday falls during the summer—that often won't work at all because everyone is on vacation or away at camp.

Your child's Hebrew birthday is a starting point. Remember that as soon as she turns thirteen, she *is* bat mitzvah. If the service which celebrates this milestone doesn't take place on the exact next Shabbat, or even later than that, it's perfectly fine. If the birthday occurs during the summer, then you can wait until the fall when everyone will be around.

Again, much depends on the policies of your synagogue, how many families they have to accommodate, and how flexible they are.

This becomes important because when you are assigned a bar mitzvah date at your synagogue, it will likely be based on your Jewish birthday.

Time for some astronomical fun. Since the Jewish calendar is lunar, the months correspond directly with the phases of the moon. In fact, this is just how people living in ancient times were able to keep track of the dates and when to celebrate the holidays and festivals. You can do the same thing in modern times! All you have to remember is that the words "moon" and "month" are pretty much the same.

Each time a new month starts, so does a new moon. Let's go back to our Rosh Hashanah example, but don't worry, I won't make you start walking on brick paths anymore. Since we know that Rosh Hashanah begins on the first day of the Jewish month, then we also know that each year on Rosh Hashanah, if you look up at the sky at night you'll see . . . not much at all.

The moon is brand new, which means that it's not visible yet. Perhaps, on the next night, you might be able to see the smallest sliver of moon in the sky. Then, as the Jewish month progresses, so does the size of the moon. But remember, the month represents one entire cycle of the moon, so during that twenty-nine or thirty days it has to go from new to full and back down to new again.

Therefore, the full moon, which of course is a lot easier to see, will always fall right in the middle of the month. It's no coincidence that a significant number of Jewish holidays take place on the 14th of the Jewish month. First, in the old days, it was easy to just look up at the moon and see when the festival began. Second, if celebrating the festival involved traveling or making a pilgrimage to Jerusalem, then it certainly was a lot easier to do that at night by the light of a full moon.

The Jewish religion is not the only major culture to use a lunar calendar. People living in ancient times, wherever they were in the world, and whatever technology or knowledge they possessed, always had one thing in common. They could all look up at the night sky and see the moon. Therefore, other groups of people used the moon to keep track of the passage of time as well.

One very well-known example is the Islamic calendar. Unlike the Jewish calendar, which is lunisolar (I love using that word), the Islamic calendar is purely lunar. For instance, one month in the Islamic calendar that you may have heard of is called Ramadan, and to devout Muslims, it is a holy month.

INSIDER'S TIP!

THE FIRST DAY of a Jewish month is actually an important day. In Hebrew this day is called *Rosh Chodesh* (literally, "head of the month"), and is treated like a mini-festival. In services on that day, there are a few different things recited (and yes, the service is just a little bit longer).

You should be aware of *Rosh Chodesh* because it might have a direct impact on your service, haftarah, and Torah reading. Whenever Shabbat and *Rosh Chodesh* come at the same time (on average, maybe a few times a year), there is a special haftarah chanted. The benefit to this is that long after your bar mitzvah is over, you will know this haftarah very well and might volunteer to chant it again for one of the many times it comes up over the years.

Of course, the cantor or rabbi at your synagogue will have checked the calendar before assigning you anything, to check for *Rosh Chodesh* or any other special occasion.

And even more moon facts: Let's talk about eclipses—both lunar and solar. The more dramatic (and rare) is a solar eclipse, when the moon passes between the earth and the sun, thus blocking out the sun for people who are at certain locations on earth.

A lunar eclipse is also pretty cool; it occurs when the earth is between the moon and sun, and therefore blocks the light from hitting the moon.

Because of where the moon is in relation to the sun, there are two facts that can never change: (1) a solar eclipse can only take place when the moon is new and (2) a lunar eclipse can only take place when the moon is full.

This means that every solar eclipse that has ever taken place in the multi-billion-year history of our solar system has fallen on *Rosh Chodesh*.

During Ramadan, many Muslims fast during the daylight hours. Since we already know that the lunar calendar is eleven days shorter than the regular calendar, Ramadan will drift eleven days earlier every year.

Over the course of many years, Ramadan, occurring eleven days earlier each year, may fall in the winter, in the summer, or any other time. I would imagine that Muslims who are fasting during the daylight hours prefer when Ramadan occurs during the winter, simply because the days are shorter.

Another example of a lunar calendar is the Chinese calendar, which also uses the moon to keep track of months. The Chinese calendar, like the Jewish calendar, is lunisolar, with an extra month added every now and then in order to keep Chinese New Year anchored to a certain time of year (January or February). But because they both are based on the moon, you always know that Chinese New Year falls on *Rosh Chodesh*—they're both the first day of the lunar month.

INSIDER'S TIP!

HERE ARE the months of the Jewish calendar in order, and when they generally occur within the regular calendar. I also listed several familiar Jewish holidays that take place within those months.

1.	Tishrei	Sept., Oct.	Rosh Hashanah, Yom Kippur
2.	Cheshvan	Oct., Nov.	
3.	Kislev	Nov., Dec.	Chanukah
4.	Tevet	Dec., Jan.	
5.	Shevat	Jan., Feb.	
6.	Adar	Feb., March	Purim
7.	Nisan	March, April	Passover
8.	Iyar	April, May	
9.	Sivan	May, June	Shavuot
10.	Tammuz	June, July	
11.	Av	July, Aug.	
12.	Elul	Aug., Sept.	

Hey, what about when there's a leap year, and an entire extra month is added? In this case, the month of Adar (#6 above) morphs into two separate months, and becomes Adar I and Adar II. Then there would actually be thirteen months in that year.

While only a few of us actually took the time to memorize all the months in order (just doing my job, ma'am), it really is helpful if you can remember a few. For instance, if you can memorize that Rosh Hashanah falls in Tishrei, Chanukah takes place in Kislev, and Passover occurs in Nisan, you'll be in very good shape.

Can We Get Some Service Here Please?

UNLESS YOU'VE been coming to temple for a long time, it can be confusing trying to figure out all the different parts of the service. To make things much more complicated, there are numerous Hebrew terms that refer to various sections of the service. I know that sometimes when I'm giving a lesson, I'll forget that the kid sitting across from me isn't a liturgical scholar, and while I'm busy saying *Shacharit* this and *Musaf* that, I completely lost him ten minutes ago and he's just too polite to let me know.

The service actually has a really logical structure and is pretty easy to appreciate with just a basic understanding. Since your bar mitzvah service is most likely to take place during a Shabbat morning, let's take a close look at how the service is set up and what it's all about.

Good Morning!

The morning service is called *Shacharit* in Hebrew. It doesn't matter if it's a Tuesday or Saturday, Rosh Hashanah or your birthday, the morning service is always called *Shacharit.*

The *Shacharit* service begins with a special section called *Birchot Hashachar*, meaning "blessings of the morning." Depending on what your temple requires you to learn for your bar mitzvah, you may or may not have to lead some or all of these prayers. Additionally, this section may be one of the more unfamiliar parts of the *Shacharit* service simply because it comes at the very beginning and many congregants and guests don't arrive until a little later.

Imagine if you had to write your own prayers. You would want to know when these prayers would be recited, and by whom, and what you should make them about. Should they be about nature? Something praising God? Perhaps some words about a specific holiday? This is information that you would need so you could compose a prayer that made sense.

OK, so here's your mission, should you choose to accept: Come up with some prayers that you think would seem sensible for first thing in the morning. They will be recited every morning of the year and will serve as an introduction to the rest of the service.

What kind of things would you include? Well, let's see. This is something that you want to be appropriate and meaningful for very early in the

INSIDER'S TIP!

THESE BLESSINGS didn't always appear in the *Siddur*. Originally, in the Talmud, they were recited privately by a person in his house.

After opening his eyes for the first time in the morning, he would say, "Blessed are you God who removes slumber from my eyelids and sleep from my eyes."

Imagine such a wonderfully appropriate text written almost two thousand years ago!

There were other actions associated with blessings as well. For instance, as soon as he swung his legs out of bed and put his feet on the floor, a person would recite a blessing praising God for making his steps firm. After standing up, another blessing would follow that thanked God for the ability to stand upright.

And so on for many more blessings.

Since that time, all of these blessings have been consolidated into one opening section for everyone to recite as part of the service. But when you understand where they came from, it really adds a lot more meaning to the text.

day, so how about some words giving thanks for a new day. Even more basic, perhaps something about being able to get out of bed. To just open your eyes after waking up!

In fact, these are precisely the kind of blessings that we read in this opening section of *Birchot Hashachar*. In most *Siddurim*, the service opens with a long list of blessings praising God for the ability to do lots of things that we might otherwise take for granted, but for which we're thankful first thing in the morning.

These include the ability to distinguish between day and night, get out of bed, be free, have clothes, and not go hungry. When you think about it, that's a nice way to start the day, isn't it?

Some Psalms

This opening section of *Birchot Hashachar* is followed by another segment called *Pesukei D'zimrah* ("verses of song"). Primarily, these pages are made up of Psalms.

Back in chapter 2 I mentioned that the Hebrew Bible, better known by its acronym *Tanakh*, is comprised of three distinct parts. The first two, *Torah* and *Nevi'im*, are where you spend most of your time during lessons, learning a haftarah or a Torah reading, depending on your synagogue. But the third section, *Ketuvim*, or Writings, includes a large book of the Bible called Psalms. There are 150 Psalms, and they are all poems or texts that praise God. Back in Temple times (that's capital T, so you know I'm talking a couple thousand years ago), the Psalms were sung as part of the worship service.

Today, we recite a lot of the Psalms in a specific order at this point in the service. Many shuls use this section as a way to save time as well. It's common for synagogues to abbreviate the *Pesukei D'zimrah* section by omitting many pages and just reciting a few "must-do" Psalms.

Within this section is Psalm 145, better known by its nickname, *Ashrei*. This is a well-known prayer, and is actually recited twice during the service. It's commonly done by bar mitzvah kids and other students, and it could even be handed out as an honor to a particularly capable guest. (Stay tuned for much more on that in chapter 8.)

INSIDER'S TIP!

THE *ASHREI* is one of several prayers that are actually written in alphabetical order (according to the Hebrew alphabet). That is to say, each subsequent line of the text begins with the next letter.

There were good reasons why prayers or Psalms would be composed like this. Mainly, it makes it a lot easier to remember the words when they're in alphabetical order. That may not be such an important deal now when every person in shul can simply pick up a *Siddur* and turn to the proper page, but think back to a time when *Siddurim* were not available, or when most people couldn't even read! They had to depend on a learned person to lead the prayers and know what to say, and they could listen and maybe hope to sing along if they knew some of the words. A prayer like *Ashrei* made that task a little bit easier.

The Call to Get Things Started

What would you think if I told you that we hadn't even really begun the service yet?

Believe it or not, the *Shacharit* service hasn't even officially begun at this point. That happens next with a prayer called *Barchu*, which is the official public call to worship. If that's the case, then what have we just spent maybe a half hour doing?

Pretend that you were about to start a rigorous session of exercise. Would you immediately jump in and just get going? I bet that you've been told that it's important to get ready first by stretching and then easing into the strenuous activity. Eventually, you'll be able to work at full effort.

Prayer is the same way! This is important stuff and we want to make sure that we're completely ready. Because we're using our minds more than our muscles, the way we "stretch" is to start reciting things that will get our attention on the right subject and get us thinking about what we want to say. Therefore, instead of just beginning the service with the really heavy material, we ease our heads into it by giving thanks for having woken up and being able to be there, as well as praising God with the words of the Psalms.

OK, enough warming up. You're ready.

The *Barchu* gets everyone started and ready to proceed with the morning service. Imagine a judge banging his gavel and calling out, "Order! Order in the court!" That's what the text of the *Barchu* is really telling us.

The *Barchu* is also noteworthy because it can only be recited if there is a *minyan* present. Remember from chapter 1 that a *minyan* refers to the presence of ten or more adult Jews at a service. Generally speaking, before you become bar mitzvah, you don't get counted in the *minyan*, but one of your new privileges as a freshly minted adult is that you are now included. This becomes really important when you have prayers like the *Barchu* that need a *minyan*.

What's so special about the *Barchu* that it requires ten or more people? In fact, there are lots of equally or even more important prayers in the *Siddur* that can be recited no matter who is there. Keep in mind that the point of the *Barchu* is to call everyone to order and get the service moving. It's the public call to worship. The main word there being "public." It wouldn't make much sense to be praying by yourself and inviting everyone to get started.

Remember that judge banging his gavel to quiet down the courtroom? Wouldn't he look really silly if he were sitting by himself in an empty room, banging his gavel and yelling, "I must have order in this court!"? How about if you were the chairman of a company and had to lead a really important meeting, but the only people to show up were you and two managers? I don't think you would stand up at your podium and formally announce, "OK everyone, it's time for us to begin this meeting."

And so it is with the *Barchu*.

Getting Ready for the Shema

Picture a river that you're trying to cross. The only way you can do it is to find big enough stones that you can use as steps in order to get across.

Our *Shacharit* service has stepping stones like this as well. They are the most important parts of the service, and the pages beforehand serve to prepare us.

The *Barchu* was the first big stone. Now we have to make our way to the next one, and that will be the *Shema*.

"You mean I actually have to learn Hebrew?!"

The *Shema* could well be the most famous and well-known text in the service. It was probably one of the very first prayers that you, and your parents, and *their* parents ever learned. It's recited not only in the service but also traditionally before going to bed, and there's also a custom that says that whenever possible, the *Shema* should be the last thing a person says before death.

The text is both familiar and simple:

Shema Yisrael, Adonai Eloheinu, Adonai Echad!
Hear, Israel, that our God is one!

What makes this so profound?

Would you believe that before this line was written, no one had ever, *ever* said that there was one God?

Judaism is a monotheistic religion, which means that we believe in one God. ("Mono" = one, "Theism" = belief in God.) That doesn't sound like such a big deal. Pretty much everyone we know—Christian, Muslim, or Jew—believes in one God, although certainly in different ways. But Judaism was the very first monotheistic religion. Before then, some people, like the ancient Egyptians and Greeks, routinely worshipped lots of gods (notice the small "g") and prayed to idols.

They might have given thanks to a sun god, for instance, and then another god who controlled the rain, and still another who saved them from disaster. It was a radical notion, never before expressed by anyone, when the Jewish people came on the scene and declared, "No! There is only One God, who controls everything."

That one line is so vital because, in just six Hebrew words, it contains the very essence of Judaism.

Wow, no wonder we had to warm up and recite a whole bunch of other prayers before we got here. You can't just jump into a prayer this weighty and meaningful.

Some Interesting Customs

When reciting the *Shema,* it's customary to close your eyes. There's no one right way to do this; some people take their hand and cover their eyes, and others simply close their eyes. Still others just keep their eyes open. It's not a law or requirement, but simply something that worshippers can do to enhance the meaning of the words.

A couple of different reasons are usually given for closing your eyes. First, it helps you to concentrate on this very important prayer. By closing your eyes, you eliminate all outside distractions and can fully focus on the words. Second, the direction is to "hear" that God is one. So we close our eyes so that we can make sure that we're literally using our ears and sense of hearing to fulfill the order to hear.

Additionally, there's an interesting custom, when reciting the words of the *Shema* out loud, of pronouncing a word in a unique way. These words come from the book of Deuteronomy, and in the Torah, are written so that the last letters of the first word, "Shema," and the last word, "Echad," are larger than the others. If we take these two letters, the Hebrew letter *ayin* and *dalet,* and put them together, we have the Hebrew word *eid,* which means "witness." It tells us that we have the responsibility, in every generation, to remember that God is one.

When we pronounce these words out loud, we overemphasize the last letter *dalet* by enunciating "echa**D**." You may hear others doing this in services as well, so that you'll have a small chorus of Ds around the sanctuary. We do this in order to remember that this word appears in the Torah with a large letter *dalet*. Another reason given for over pronouncing the D sound is to make sure we don't mistake the *dalet* for its look-alike Hebrew letter *resh*, which would turn the word *echad* ("one") into *acher* ("another"). "Hear, Israel, that our God is another" just doesn't have the same ring to it.

Take a Stand

The next major stepping stone in the service is called the *Amidah*, or "standing prayer." Because the *Amidah* is so important, you can't have a service without it. No matter what service you're talking about, regardless of time of day or whatever holiday it might be, it will contain an *Amidah*. In fact, when the rabbis of the Talmud wanted to refer to the *Amidah*, they would just use the word *tefilah*, meaning "prayer." In modern Hebrew, that word can refer to any text at all in the *Siddur*, but it shows how basic the *Amidah* is to the service. Every *Amidah* begins exactly the same way, but then it changes depending on whether it's Shabbat (the most likely case for your bar mitzvah) or a weekday, or some other holiday.

The *Amidah* is sometimes referred to as the *Shmoneh Esrei*, which literally means "eighteen." Originally, the weekday *Amidah* contained eighteen blessings. Then somewhere along the way, one more was added at the end, but since the name *Shmoneh Esrei* had already caught on, no one bothered to call it anything different. To make matters even more confusing, the Shabbat version only contains seven blessings. That's why I like to call it the *Amidah* and make it as simple as possible.

There are also various ways that the *Amidah* can be recited, and your temple will have its own usual way. The most traditional of these is to recite the entire prayer silently, wait for everyone to be done (or at least give a reasonable amount of time for most to finish), and then to start back at the beginning and chant it all out loud. This is a throwback to an earlier time before it was common for every member of a congregation to have a *Siddur*. The *Amidah* is so important that we want to make sure that everyone has a chance to either recite it properly or even just hear it and respond "Amen" to its blessings.

Since most worshippers now have access to a *Siddur*, and can certainly read the English if they don't know how to read Hebrew, other customs have developed. In order to save time (and keep the congregation a little more engaged), we often begin the *Amidah* out loud together and sing through the first part. Then we continue the rest silently and just go on with the service. In some congregations, the entire *Amidah* is recited out loud. I like having at least part of the *Amidah* recited silently, because it's a good opportunity for a little quiet time, and it's appropriate for everyone present to add their own personal prayers.

Like other parts of the service, some interesting choreography goes along with the *Amidah*. Just before you begin, it's customary to take three small steps backward, and then three steps forward. Then while you're reciting the *Amidah*, you stand with your feet together. Finally, when you're all done, you take three small steps back.

To help understand why we do this rather strange sounding custom, imagine that you've been invited to have an audience with a really important king or queen. (And really, what king or queen *isn't* important?) So there you are, dressed up nicely, on your best behavior, and you're shown into the royal chamber. It's a beautiful room, marble floors, ornate decorations all over, and way in the distance you see the king sitting on his throne, waiting for you to come over and be recognized. It certainly wouldn't look very good if you sort of shuffled over, or took your time getting there. Instead, you'd stand up straight, and make your way directly to the throne.

Then, when you were done, it would be pretty disrespectful to the king if you said, "Hey, thanks a lot, King, have a nice day," turned your back on him, and left the room. Instead, you would probably be better off backing out gracefully, not showing him your back, and exiting the chamber that way.

Now, if we give a human king that much respect, we should show even more to God when we're praying! Therefore, during the *Amidah*, which is just like the one-on-one conversation that I described with that king, we try to do the same kind of thing. We begin by taking three steps forward in order to approach God with respect, stand still with our feet not moving all over the place, and then back out with a sense of deference. This is an example of how our movements can really help us get in the right frame of mind, and make sure that we're in the proper mood for a certain prayer.

Here Comes the Torah

And now we get to the real heart of the service. All of these important stepping stones have been leading us to the main event—namely, taking out the Torah and getting ready for the reading.

I always thought it would be really cool to be the President of the United States, because the guy's got his own theme song. Every time he walks into a room, one of the military bands starts playing "Hail to the Chief" and everybody stands up. (That must get really annoying at 3:00 in the morning when he has trouble sleeping and walks into the other room to read a book.)

We treat the Torah with the same sort of reverence. Each time the Torah is taken out of the ark, everyone stands out of respect and we sing a special prayer. We carry the Torah around the congregation so that everyone present has the opportunity to see it up close. It's customary to touch the Torah with the corner of your *tallit,* or your *Siddur,* or even your fingers, and then give that item a kiss.

Because the Torah is considered to be so sacred, we stand out of respect anytime the Torah is raised, lifted, or even just moved from one place to another.

INSIDER'S TIP!

Y OU WILL likely be the one who gets to carry the Torah around in this little processional. Please do everyone a favor and take your time when you're walking. It looks pretty funny when the bat mitzvah kid takes off with the Torah down the aisle and the poor congregants start lunging quickly toward the center trying to touch the Torah before it races by.

In most places, the cantor and rabbi will be walking behind you and can help "remind" you to slow down a bit. (I find a hand on the shoulder does the trick nicely.) Just remember that this is everyone's chance to come in contact with the Torah, so even though you might be trying to get the service over with a couple minutes sooner, you should slow down a bit and take your time.

Back on the *bimah,* after the Torah is put down on the *amud* (lectern) and everyone has sat down, we continue with the actual Torah reading. This is described in detail in other chapters, but you should realize that it's no accident that this part of the service takes place pretty much right in the middle. It's literally the central part of the Shabbat service. So far we've warmed up a little (*Birchot Hashachar* and *Pesukei D'zimrah*), called everyone to order to get things started (*Barchu*), announced the one, vital belief of Judaism (*Shema*), and recited the main prayer of the service (the *Amidah*).

I like to think that we've spent all this time talking to God; now it's God's turn to talk to us, through the words of the Torah. In addition to the actual reading, this is a popular time for the rabbi to give an explanation of that week's Torah portion. It's also possible that you will be the one to give that talk, with the speech that you prepared. This is often the part of the service that congregants look forward to the most, precisely because it's different every week. We can assume all the prayers are mostly the same every time, but the Torah portion changes each week, and it's interesting to hear what that week's reading will be on.

After the Torah reading is completed, we have a special way to lift and dress the Torah scroll and put it aside until we're ready to replace it in the ark. Next comes the haftarah, which you may have spent, oh, I don't know, maybe *months* preparing. After that's over, it's time to put the Torah away. So cue the special song, everyone stands up, and you walk (not run) around the sanctuary again as you make your way back up to the *bimah* so we can return the Torah scroll to its place in the ark.

Are We Done Yet?

It would certainly seem like we should be. If you keep in mind the stepping stone image, then it sure feels like we've made our way across the river. Can't you just taste the lunch at this point?

Alas, not so fast. Depending on your synagogue, you probably have one more piece of the service to get through. This would be the *Musaf,* or "additional" service. In the old days (and I mean *really* old days), before we had synagogues and prayer books and rabbis and bagels and cream cheese, the way that people observed Judaism was to bring animals to be sacrificed in the Temple (yes, capital T) in Jerusalem. The *Musaf* service recalls this time. And because it's considered a whole separate service (even though it's pretty short and is tacked on directly to the *Shacharit*), there's another *Amidah*. Remember, you can't have a service without one.

The text is kind of tricky and presents us modern Jews with a challenge. In the traditional version, we not only remember these animal sacrifices, but pray for a return to those times, when the Temple will be rebuilt in Jerusalem and we'll all have a chance to resume the routine of sacrifices. Now, I love a good barbeque as much as the next person, but are these really the wishes that we want to be praying?

Modern editions of this text have changed the wording to reflect more of a historic remembrance of those times, rather than a desire to go back, which I think makes a lot of sense. *Musaf* then becomes what I like to think of as a "snapshot" service—just like a picture, it captures one important moment in time that we revisit and think about. Sure, we don't sacrifice animals now, but why did the Jewish people do that a couple thousand years ago? What were they thinking? What commandments were they fulfilling? How do we tap into that same feeling, but without committing mass bovicide?

Like other parts of the service that may be considered too ancient for modern minds, the *Musaf* may not be included in some congregations. In any case, it's pretty short and doesn't last too long.

Are We Done Now?

Yup, pretty much. There will be some closing songs, and probably some announcements for the synagogue, and assorted things like that.

The Bottom Line

It really helps to understand the service isn't just a random collection of prayers, most of which you don't understand and can't wait to end.

Instead, it works like a good symphony. It begins with some ideas, which then get expanded upon, and moves from one main idea to the next. It has distinct movements, each with its own mood and characteristics. Afterward, the service doesn't just end abruptly but rather takes you down and eases you out of the experience.

When you understand each section, and what its purpose is, it makes it so much more meaningful and easy to connect.

CHAPTER 6

What If I Make a Mistake?!

THIS IS PROBABLY your all-time nightmare. You're standing up on the *bimah*, in front of all your friends and family, all dressed up, *tallit* perfectly set on your shoulders, chanting away just like you practiced, when all of a sudden . . . *you make a mistake!*

Oh, the HORROR!

I've had so many students do a fantastic job at their b'nei mitzvah—they were practiced, smooth, their pace was good—and all they could fixate on was the *one page* where they sang the wrong melody. I'm not exaggerating. I remember one student who, every single time a friend or relative would congratulate her, would say, "Oh, but I messed up on page 86." Now, it's nice to strive to do a good job, but this is getting carried away. After months and months of lessons and practicing, and finally having it all pay off so well on the day of the bat mitzvah, all this kid can think about is the one mistake that she made. And I bet years from now, when she remembers her bat mitzvah ceremony, she'll still recall the page where she . . . *gasp* . . . sang the wrong tune.

This student is actually pretty typical. Listen—it's human nature to worry what people are going to think, and let's face it, your average thirteen-year-old doesn't possess a great deal of self-esteem to begin with. So let's take a moment to sort things out. In this chapter we'll go over all the mistakes, errors, mishaps, nightmares, and other assorted missteps that you're already imagining—and then figure out that none of them is so bad at all.

Assuming you want to do a good job at your bar mitzvah, why is that? What's your goal? Or as they say in show biz, what's your motivation?

The Curse of the Well-Meaning Parent (a Whole Section Just for Parents)

OK, parents, admit it. At one point you've told your nervous kid, "It's all right if you make a mistake; no one understands what you're singing anyway."

Is that supposed to be helpful?

Here is what you're really telling your child: Any member of the congregation who might happen to understand a few words of Hebrew will think that you're a total moron, but thank goodness that the majority won't have a clue what you're doing. Or, to take it a step further, all these strange words and melodies that you have to memorize don't mean anything—not to you, not to the congregation, not to anyone. Just memorize everything and pray that no one knows what you're doing.

Mom and Dad, I know you're trying to be helpful, I really do. But please, please stop telling your kid that it's OK to make a mistake because no one knows what he's singing anyway. Instead, tell him it's OK to make a mistake because he's thirteen years old and no one in the world would ever expect him to be perfect.

While we're at it, here are a couple more bits of advice that you've probably told your child—but you shouldn't!

Look up and make eye contact occasionally while you're singing or speaking

No! Don't do it! You may have made this suggestion, but I already instructed your child not to look up even if the building is on fire.

Let's pretend the bar mitzvah boy does look up—what do you think he's going to see? That's right, Uncle Jerry in the front row. You remember Jerry—he's the one who thinks it's funny to put straws in his nose at family dinners and pretend he's a walrus. Jerry also chooses this time to cross his eyes and puff out his cheeks when he sees his nephew looking up.

Every family has an Uncle Jerry.

It's also likely that all of his friends who are sitting there bored out of their minds waiting for the party to start are also waiting . . . hoping . . . for just one chance to make him laugh.

And on an even more practical note, when you look up, you have a much greater tendency to lose your place or get distracted from what you're doing. Keeping your eyes on the page lets you focus more effectively.

That may be fine, you're thinking, during the service or chanting of the haftarah. What about when your son or daughter is delivering a speech or *d'var Torah*? Don't you have to look up occasionally and make eye contact during that time? Isn't that basic etiquette for public speaking?

The answer is yes. And I'm still going to advise against it.

In my experience, there's just something somewhat funny looking about a thirteen-year-old kid standing at a podium and trying to deliver a speech as if he were forty-five years old. There's still too much risk of getting distracted, making eye contact with the wrong people, and losing his place on the paper.

Of course, he should never lean way down, with his face practically on his sheet and say, "thankyouallforcomingthankyoutomyparentsforalltheir-supportandmylittlebrotherfornotbuggingmewhileIwaspracticing."

There's a nice, comfortable middle ground, when the kid speaks clearly, has his face visible to the congregation, but is still keeping his eyes on what he's reading. It will look and sound natural.

Slow down when you sing

Not bad advice really, but I have to say: Give it up, Mom and Dad. It's just not going to happen.

Here's why: You have a nervous thirteen-year-old up there just doing her best to remember how to sing and pronounce each word, what page to turn to, and where to go for the next thing. Nervous kids (and adults) sing and speak quickly. I can remind, nag, and cajole a kid all day long to slow down a little, but in two minutes, they're back to their normal pace.

That's right—what sounds fast to us is just normal to them.

So let them be normal. In the long run, they'll come across much more natural than if they're artificially trying to slooooooow waaaaaaay dooooooooown.

Mistakes Are Actually Perfectly OK

Mistakes are OK because . . . are you ready? Here it comes . . . *everyone makes mistakes!* Do you think your bar mitzvah training includes how to be a robot? Do you think you're in the God-training program? When I tell my students this idea, they invariably give me the response, "Cantor, that's easy for you to say. You're the cantor. You never make mistakes in the service."

That's unbelievably funny to me. I make mistakes all the time. I've garbled words. I've forgotten melodies. I've lost my place in the text. My voice has cracked in the middle of a solo, making me sound like a fifteen-year-old whose voice is changing. Once a fly kept trying to land on my nose (admittedly not an insignificant target), while I tried in vain to be really cool and just give a few swats to keep it away. And if all that's not bad enough, I happen to work with a rabbi who tries to make me laugh just to see if he can. (No, his name is not Uncle Jerry.)

When I point out to my students that, in fact, I mess up all the time, I get this line: "OK, but you're the cantor. No one knows that you've made a mistake."

Not true—they do know. They just don't really care.

Now you're getting the idea.

I'm sure some people notice a mispronounced word, and many do not. It really doesn't matter. What's important is that I'm able to act as if everything is just fine and simply go on with the service. I don't make a big deal out of every error, scrunching up my face, looking dejected, and I certainly don't respond to a congregant's "Shabbat Shalom" with "Did you hear how I messed up on page 157?"

One facet of bar mitzvah preparation that drives my students crazy is when I insist that they *learn how to make a mistake.* But it's a skill that's really important and will also serve you well in lots of other areas.

Let's take a student who is almost finished with her training. She knows her haftarah really well and has been practicing and working very hard. We're in the run-through stage now, which means that my job is to sit back and relax and let her sing all the way through just to hear how it all sounds, and so she can get a feel for what it will be like to stand there and sing at her bat mitzvah.

As the student sings through a portion of it, she gets hung up on a word. I don't know why—maybe the vowels just got the best of her that time. Anyway, she tries to get the word correctly, stumbles and stutters her way through it, and finally stops and says, "I can't get this word."

She wants me to help her with the word, of course. Instead, I ask, "At your bat mitzvah, are you going to stop and announce that you can't get this word? What would you really do when this happens?" (Notice I said "when" and not "if.")

Take another common situation. A student is chanting his haftarah, which he knows well, when he stops after every word he wasn't 100 percent sure of and asks, "Was that right?"

Bar mitzvah preparation is intended to accomplish a couple of things. The obvious goal is to teach you all the material that you need to know.

INSIDER'S TIP!

'LL SHARE another secret with you. Kids who chant all the way through without ever making the slightest mistake whatsoever don't sound natural. Now, of course, it's not a hard and fast rule, and I certainly wouldn't want to give the impression that you should try to make mistakes. But sometimes kids have memorized everything to such an extreme degree that it sounds too practiced, too memorized.

If you're not sure what I mean, consider this scenario:

Let's pretend that you had to stand up in front of a large audience and deliver a speech (which, incidentally, is pretty much every adult's most dreaded fear). The topic of the speech is actually not something that you're an expert on, so you write out the entire speech to make sure that it's OK. Then you practice your way through the speech. You read it many times over and over. You put little notations on the paper where you should pause, or where you might stress a word. Eventually, you've got it perfect.

When you deliver it, though, it's still going to sound like you're reading a bunch of pages into the microphone.

I've found that the kids who sounded the best at their bar mitzvah services were the ones who sounded natural—occasional mistakes and all.

(How much material will vary depending upon what kind of synagogue you're in.) The other goal is to teach you how to get up on the *bimah* and have the presence of a Jewish adult. Or possibly to just give you your first real chance to try some public speaking. Whether it's something that you actually don't mind, or it's your worst nightmare, it's something that everyone has to do sooner or later, so you might as well have some real practice.

It's perfectly acceptable to make an occasional mistake—what's really important is to keep going. Sure, if you make a quick stumble it's appropriate to fix it and move on. But most of the time kids get all messed up when they try to go back and get a certain word to sound that perfect way that they memorized. In the meantime, they've brought the service to a crashing halt. And by the way, here's the ironic part: If you're really so concerned with everyone noticing your every mistake, the best way to call attention to it is to stop and stumble over a word. Even non-Jewish guests sitting in the congregation realize you've made an error when that happens.

When my students are at the point where they really know the haftarah or whatever prayer we're working on very well, I tell them to just sing through it. Don't stop. Don't ask if it was right. Don't spend twenty seconds trying to pronounce one word. Sometimes, I might stop them to work on something, but if I'm silent, they should keep on going. The idea isn't to learn how to be perfect but rather how to stand up in front of a congregation and lead a portion of the service.

Do you remember when I started this section with the question "What's your goal?"

It's not to get up on the *bimah* and sound like a little robot. The idea is to show that you're able to lead a part of the service, or chant a Torah reading or haftarah like any other "regular" Jew.

Other Things That Could Go Wrong

I know what you're thinking: Why in the world would I devote an entire section to worst-case scenarios?

The answer is that the reality is far, far less daunting than what you're already thinking in your head. So let's get it all out there so we can see that in the light of day, these possibilities that you consider nightmares are not really a big deal.

Nightmare Scenario #1: You'll forget the tune

In fact, I'd be surprised if you didn't forget something. Also, to make things even more confusing, a lot of the same prayers have different melodies depending on when they occur in the service. So you might very well remember something just fine, and then sing it at the wrong time.

If that happens, and you realize it with horror after you've already started, just go with the flow. Usually the cantor or rabbi who is up on the *bimah* with you is way ahead of you, and already knows that you sang *this* when you meant to sing *that*. Often we're able to intervene in a subtle way and redirect the tune. Or we'll just sing the wrong tune!

Nightmare Scenario #2: You're leading a service and you think that you'll come in at the wrong time

This actually requires some explanation.

If you've ever been to a service, especially in a more traditional setting, then you know that there's a rhythm, a flow to the prayers. A typical set-up is such that the cantor or other person leading the service will begin a paragraph or section out loud, followed by everyone continuing with silent reading, and concluding with the cantor finishing the paragraph by chanting the last few lines out loud.

How does a typical bar mitzvah kid know when to come back in at the end? How can he tell that the congregation is done with the silent reading?

I'm going to give you two answers—the longer, correct, cantorial, and adult answer that parents will approve of, and the short one that you want to hear.

First the easy answer: Just listen. The term "silent reading" is actually a misnomer; there's really nothing silent about it at all. You often hear a lot of worshippers making a mumbling noise as they read the words to themselves. Plus, when people get to the last few words, they often end them just a little louder. So in a real service, you'll actually hear congregants, and most likely the rabbi and cantor, reading silently. As a result, it's not that hard to figure out when it's your turn to come back in and conclude the paragraph.

Now the more difficult answer: You shouldn't need the answer I just gave you, because it assumes that the service is something that is going on around you. You're not a part of it, but rather some actor who wandered onto the wrong stage, looking at a script where you have no idea what the plot is and what the other actors are doing, and you have to somehow deliver your lines at the proper time. Looking at it from that perspective, no wonder you're so nervous!

But luckily that's not the case. When you are standing at that podium on the *bimah*, the service isn't just taking place, but rather *you are leading the service*. That's actually a pretty hefty burden. There are congregants sitting in the sanctuary who are trying to fulfill their obligation to pray—they're depending on you for that. This is also why we only allow adults (ahem . . . that's you) to lead services.

So if you're just standing up there in blissful ignorance of everything going on *except* for your next cue so you can deliver the next line of script . . . well, that's sort of missing the point, isn't it?

Again, remember when I started things off by asking, "What's your goal?"

Here's another answer: to get a feel for what it's like to really lead a service.

That means when there's a part of the service that is read silently, *you* should read silently too. I wish I could fully express to you how ridiculous it looks when a bar mitzvah boy stands on the *bimah*, chants a certain line, flips way ahead to his next entrance, and then spends the remaining time looking around, smiling at his friends and family, and waiting patiently for his "turn."

Yes, of course I know that many kids are not able to read Hebrew fast enough to keep up the pace. So just read a little. Or read the English. Or even just *think* about the prayers. Remember that you are *leading* the service. And if you're still wondering about knowing when to come in at the proper time if you're busy reading and trying to figure out the Hebrew, go back to my first answer. You'll hear the pace of the silent readings, so even if you weren't able to complete much of the paragraph to yourself, you can still go on.

And in the process, you'll look much more authentic and professional. Believe me that the congregation can see perfectly well which kids are taking the service more seriously and which are just sort of looking around and making faces at Uncle Jerry.

Many b'nei mitzvah tutors will mark the pages that are sung out loud, and then "helpfully" place a paper clip or something over the pages that the student will not be leading at all. This is presumably to ease the burden of remembering where to come in and what to do next.

But here's the message that it really sends: The prayer book that you're holding is actually a script for a really big play, but you only appear in certain scenes. Don't worry about the scenes where you're not on stage. No one cares about those. Furthermore, for *your* scenes, here are your lines, and here are the cues that you will hear to tell you when to recite your lines. It doesn't matter what the play is about or what each character is saying—just recite your lines in this precise way at the proper time, and the play will be presented perfectly.

(Fast forward a few years: "Hey, what do you remember about your bar mitzvah?" "Not much. I forgot all my lines.")

Instead, follow the service. Even those parts that do not directly involve you. If the service does feel like a big play, then at least try to follow the plot.

Nightmare Scenario #3: You'll faint

It is very, very unlikely that you'll faint during your bar mitzvah, or that you'll throw up, or have some other awful accident involving bodily functions.

But that being said, I guess it is theoretically possible. In all my years of working with b'nei mitzvah kids and being present at the services, it has happened only on very rare occasions. It is such a negligible possibility that it's not worth worrying about.

In my shul, we require the kids to also learn and then lead a Thursday morning *minyan* (remember the definition? "small service"). Yes, it's a little more to learn, but it's a great opportunity for a very nervous kid to lead an informal service in front of a small number of people. Often, the student will make one of those minor mistakes that I've talked about and realize, "Wow, that wasn't as bad as I thought it would be!"

It's just a nice way to get some pre–bar mitzvah jitters out in a low stress setting.

During one such Thursday morning *minyan* early in my career, in the middle of a part that was supposed to be chanted out loud, the kid wasn't singing. As I looked up, I saw her start to slump and then down she went. I was freaked out! I had never seen anyone faint before! The parents jumped up, and we all rushed over.

Meanwhile, one of the congregants who was in attendance was a doctor (imagine that!), who calmly came over, told us to just let her lie there for a second, and maybe elevate her feet just a little to get the blood back up where it belonged. We eventually got her sitting up, someone got her some water to sip, and the service went on.

Don't worry about something that is extremely unlikely. Make sure you eat something the morning of your bar mitzvah, and not last night's sushi.

Nightmare Scenario #4: You'll drop the Torah

Of course I had to include this one. It's the granddaddy of all fears. I can't imagine any bar mitzvah child (and probably quite a few parents) who hasn't had this particular worry cross his mind at least a few times.

And isn't this the time when the annoying little brother says, "Be careful you don't drop the Torah or we'll all have to fast for forty days!"

So let's play it out and expose this specific nightmare to the light.

First, you should know that *dropping a Torah scroll is extremely rare!* I personally have never witnessed such a thing happening.

You will undoubtedly get the opportunity to practice holding one and walking around with it. I will let a bat mitzvah student actually bring in the fancy shoes she'll be wearing, so she can put them on and feel what it will be like to walk down the stairs in heels while holding the Torah.

Think about it—have you ever heard of this actually happening? Sure, everyone talks about it, but have you seen it? If it were really something we worried about, surely we'd have Torah scrolls dropping all over the country. But in fact kids and adults are pretty careful when they hold the Torah, and we cantors and rabbis make sure that you're holding it securely before we let go.

But I have to address the "fasting for forty days" thing. Yes and no. Mostly no. It sounds ridiculous because it is—do you really think a person can fast for forty days? Most Jewish people I know get antsy when they have to wait two hours for the service to end so they can eat lunch.

This "law" has its basis in an old text that directed those who witnessed a Torah scroll fall to the ground to fast during the daylight hours for forty days. (Meaning, if you do actually drop a Torah, then December would be much better than July because the days are shorter. And if you should happen to have this mishap in Alaska during the summer months, well, good luck.) The text doesn't even specify that the forty days have to be in a row. And furthermore, giving *tzedakah*, or charity, may be substituted for fasting.

On those very rare occasions that I have heard that a Torah scroll was dropped (and I can count those times on one hand and still have a couple fingers and thumb left over), those who were there were simply told to donate charity out of respect for the Torah.

Realistically, don't worry about it!

The Bottom Line

All this talk of mistakes, how to make them, and that you shouldn't worry about making them might be giving you the wrong idea. You may think that when it comes to doing your bar mitzvah service and singing through the prayers and haftarah, you can relax and think, "Whatever!"

Not true at all.

You should be at least a little nervous. If you were completely casual about the whole thing, I would think that you weren't taking it seriously. I certainly get nervous whenever I have to do something unfamiliar for the first time. But the very best antidote for nervousness is being well prepared.

If you've done a lot of preparation and practice, then things are going to go very smoothly and a few missteps or mangled words aren't going to affect the big picture at all. The idea isn't to ace everything flawlessly. It's to look at a seemingly HUGE hurdle and to chip away at it, little by little, line by line if necessary, until you can stand up in front of the congregation and take part in the service as a Jewish adult. That means if your *very best effort* involves having trouble with page 96 and accidentally singing the wrong tune, and maybe switching a few vowels, that's OK. You should be incredibly proud of what you accomplished and, even more importantly, remember how it felt, because sometime in your future, there will be another HUGE hurdle. You'll know that you can handle it, because you have this experience under your belt.

And that's a much better feeling than thinking you got away with a couple mistakes because no one knew what you were singing anyway.

CHAPTER 7

You Need to Attend Services More

THIS IS NOT your typical the-cantor-says-I-need-to-attend-services-more-often chapter. The fact is that many families do not attend services at their synagogue very often. Many only come on the High Holidays. As much as we Jewish professionals would love to see more members of the congregation attend frequently, that's just the way it's always been.

The point of this chapter, then, is not to make you feel guilty or imply that you're a bad Jew. It's not to add one more obligation to your list of stuff to do when you're already loaded down with a million things. Rather, it's to give you a way to make your preparation *easier* and to help create a more pleasant experience all around.

And yes, all you have to do is come to services more often.

I believe it was Rabbi Bill Shakespeare who once said, "All the world's a stage, and the men and women merely players." He must have been talking about bar mitzvah kids.

Everyone will tell you that leading services and chanting your haftarah is not about performing but rather about praying, taking on Jewish obligations, and becoming a member of the congregation. They're right. But just for now, maybe just for this chapter, let me suggest to you that your bar mitzvah can in fact be compared to a performance.

Let's really go wild here and imagine that, instead of a service, you are really preparing to star in a popular musical on Broadway!

We'll call it: *Katz*

(Excuse me, ma'am. Yes, you, sitting in the recliner in suburban St. Louis. I'd like to thank you for chuckling. My editor wanted me to take that out and I convinced her that someone *would get it. Thanks for being the one.)*

Moving right along. How about something straightforward like this:

Bar Mitzvah: The Musical

Excellent. In order to really stage this thing, we'll need a director, a theater, costume designer, your fellow actors, and most important, the star.

Some of that is pretty easy. The theater is taken care of; the "show" will be performed in the temple. The directors will be the rabbi and cantor, and your parents can mostly take care of the costume design. (That means dragging you suit or dress shopping.) And of course, *you* will be the star of the musical.

Having participated in my own share of high school musicals (before those words were capitalized and referred to a series of movies), I remember that each actor had a bunch of major responsibilities. You were required to memorize your entrances and exits on stage, your lines, the choreography, and the actual songs, including the music and lyrics. That is definitely a lot of things to keep track of!

Your bar mitzvah service can be looked at in the same way. Luckily, you have one incredible advantage over most performers who have to get up on stage and perform in a musical.

JUST FOR PARENTS

COMPARING A bar mitzvah service to a Broadway musical could be considered the wrong message. And frankly, the last thing I ever really want a student to think is that she is the "star of the show," because, of course, it's not really a show. Indeed, in the last chapter I pointed out that the service is *not* a play and that learning and singing all the required prayers consisted of so much more than just memorizing and reciting lines in a play.

But just for this chapter, I want you to suspend disbelief and pretend that the service is a big play and the congregation is like the audience.

This is just a fun way to think about preparation and performing in a way that everyone can understand.

You get to watch the exact same production week after week, as many times as you like.

Take a moment and think about that amazing little tidbit. It's the most obvious, common-sense, slap-yourself-in-the-forehead fact that I can give you, and yet countless students and families *never* take advantage of it.

Assuming that you're the star of *Bar Mitzvah: The Musical*, you're understandably nervous about starring in your big role, you're scared about how you'll do, and you have a ton of questions about how to recite your lines, when to make entrances and exits, how to move at certain places, and a myriad of other subjects. If you were really getting ready for a play, you'd rehearse a lot on stage and eventually have a dress rehearsal before the big day.

For our production, though, you've got one major advantage over that: Your temple probably puts on a bar mitzvah almost every week. Sure, it'll depend on where you belong. Some synagogues have fewer kids, so there may be fewer b'nei mitzvah celebrated during the year. Other shuls have one every single week. The point is that you have the opportunity to watch this show, with someone else in the starring role, many times before you have to do it. And, of course, even if there's no bar mitzvah scheduled, there is certainly a service going on, which will give you almost all of the same information.

Don't be a guest at your own bar mitzvah! So many families walk into temple on the morning of the bar mitzvah looking around confused and mystified, not knowing where to sit, or even which *Siddur* we use on Saturday morning. Of course, these are all legitimate and logical questions to have—but you should learn the answers way before the morning of your bat mitzvah.

This has nothing to do with religious observance, believing in God, agreeing with the prayers, knowing Hebrew, liking the cantor, rabbi, or temple president, or any of the thousand reasons (some of them perfectly reasonable) that you don't come to services. This is all about an easy, practical way that your whole family can nail down a bravura performance. And isn't that why you're reading this in the first place?

Come to shul more. Learn the service and what goes on. See who's moving where, and who's singing what.

Let's take a close look at all the items that you'll be watching and learning as you get ready to star in your production.

CHAPTER 7

Entrances and Exits

Every synagogue is different. In one shul, you may spend the entire service on the *bimah*, the pulpit in front of the congregation. The *bimah* really is like a stage (and in fact the Hebrew word for stage is *bamah*), because most of the action takes place up there. There may be times when you have to leave the *bimah* and walk around the congregation, or move from one side to the other.

The custom in some shuls may be that you are seated with your family in the congregation (or in our pretend musical world, the audience) for part of the service and have to make a grand entrance onto the *bimah* only at a certain point. Similarly, it's possible that after you have chanted your Torah portion, haftarah, or other prayers, you would exit the *bimah* and sit back down.

You can think of each section of the service, and really, every page in the *Siddur*, the prayer book, as a separate scene. Just like in a play, many scenes will have actors entering and exiting. There have been many, many times that a bar mitzvah kid, during the service, whispers to me, "Where do I go now?" or "Why is that person coming up and what's he going to do?" These are all important entrances and exits that different "characters" have during this production.

Your Lines

Imagine that the *Siddur*, the prayer book that you will be holding, is really a script. It has everyone's part in it for our musical production. Like any script, it includes lines that you say as well as many words spoken by the other "actors." To make things yet more complicated, in this play, some of the lines are actually *not spoken at all*. They are recited silently. Finally some of your lines won't even come out of the *Siddur*. You'll most likely have to deliver a speech or *d'var Torah* (short explanation of the Torah reading or haftarah). Consider this like a scene where you're the only character on stage and you're delivering a lengthy monologue.

Since you're trying to be a really good actor, you need to not only know all your lines but also understand your *motivation*. That's a well-known acting term that refers to what an actor should be thinking about while the play is going on. For instance, if an actor were in a scene where his character just won a million dollars in the lottery, he would have to say his lines in a way that would convince the audience that he was overjoyed about winning so much money. His motivation would be his new-found wealth.

What's your motivation? That's a hard question to answer since there's a very good chance you just don't understand the play you're starring in. After all, most of the lines are in a language that you don't speak! There are some different ways you can approach this problem.

You could look at the play as a whole unit. What should you be thinking about the entire time? This answer might go through several changes. Perhaps your motivation is relief—you can't believe you're finally getting to perform this play after all the hard work you put into the preparation.

Another possibility for your motivation is responsibility. You're aware that for the very first time, you have a new obligation to perform certain rituals and Jewish commandments. At some point (probably around the time you move out of your parents' house), that will also include having the choice about which rituals you will observe. Maybe you'll keep kosher, and maybe not. Maybe you'll decide to attend a temple, put a *mezuzah* on your door, light Chanukah candles, or a million other things. Realize that as you go through life and make these very adult decisions, it can all be traced back to this day. So yeah, that's a lot of responsibility.

A different way of looking at things isn't this "big picture" view but rather concentrating more on the prayers that you're doing at that time. If you can figure out what some of the prayers are actually about, that's a great way to figure out your motivation. Is it a prayer asking for something? Are they words of praise? Something dramatic, like the beginning of the service where we take the Torah out of the ark for the first time? You will come across like a prepared, professional actor if you're reciting your lines and know how your character is supposed to feel during that scene.

One of the ways in which otherwise well-meaning bar mitzvah tutors do their students a disservice is the old paper clip trick, which I mentioned in the last chapter. A supposedly helpful teacher will notice that a student is not required to lead a certain section of the service, so she will clip all those pages together, so that the student can easily flip from the end of one section that he's singing directly to his next pages, all the while forgetting about the pages that are clipped shut.

What happens to those pages? Who's doing those lines? What are they? What's going on in the play? The problem with this approach is that it prevents you from really developing the proper motivation, since you aren't

INSIDER'S TIP!

MANY PARTS of the Torah, as well as the haftarot (plural for haftarah), are actually very interesting stories, and you will undoubtedly have the opportunity to learn what yours is about during the course of lessons. When you're chanting your Torah reading or haftarah, you're really telling the audience a story. Your motivation will be influenced by knowing all about that story.

For example, some of the stories that we read in the different haftarot are *really* action packed, and if someone decided to make them into a movie, they'd be filled with lots of violence and romance—in other words, just the kind of movie that you're probably used to seeing!

One famous story has the heroine lulling the bad guy into a false sense of security by pretending to be romantically interested. When he's not paying attention, she sneaks up on him and stabs him through the head with a spear. (Judges 4:21)

Another haftarah describes how one of the kings of Israel (who, by the way, was manic depressive) did not follow God's directions and kill the opposing king of an evil tribe after wiping out everyone else. As a punishment, his family was forever stripped of royalty, and he lived out the rest of his life in shame. (I Samuel 15:7–23)

Still another story describes how the Israelites snuck into a town, aided by a local lady-of-the-evening, and were able to ambush the enemy Canaanites. (Joshua 2)

These stories are compelling, filled with action, and resonate powerfully to modern audiences. Are you describing a quiet, nature-filled scene, or a violent and bloody episode? The more you make an effort to understand the words you're singing (with the help of your cantor or other teacher), the better you'll come across to the congregation. It can be a subtle difference, but will go a long way toward giving you the right motivation.

actually paying attention to anything going on in the service that doesn't involve you.

There's a comparison for this in the theater world as well. Actors sometimes learn their lines using a special kind of script called a "side." Whereas a regular script will have all the lines and action for every character, and can be read through from start to finish, sides only contain the dialogue and directions for one character. They usually contain the cue lines so the actor knows what to listen for and when to come in. They're effective for memorizing lines without carrying around an entire script, but they don't really tell the actor what the play is about, or what any other character is doing or thinking. In other words, an effective actor cannot develop the proper motivation for his character by relying only on his specific lines without knowing what else might be going on.

It's important that you don't turn your prayer book into a side. You can very easily keep track of your scenes while being aware that other characters have important parts as well.

Sure, when you're just learning things during lessons, it's perfectly normal and appropriate for you to skip around to different pages, do things out of order, and not really get the feel for what the whole service is like. Your teacher may ask you to sing page 100, then go back to page 65, and finally turn all the way to the end of the service to practice something there. Obviously, you won't be concentrating too much on your motivation at this point. This is how actors practice for their performances as well; they run through various scenes out of order to rehearse their lines or other actions. It's when the whole thing is put together from start to finish that you can begin to think about what you should be feeling.

The Choreography

Right about now, you're asking yourself, "Wait, I have to dance too?" No, that's not the kind of choreography that I'm talking about. Rather, I'm referring to all the different movements that you make with your body during the service. Some choreography will be done by both you and the congregation, whereas other actions are done by you alone.

I always like to point out that at a traditional Jewish service, no one ever really stands still or reads silently. There's always some action, movement, or sound taking place. When reading silently, the traditional worshipper still will read some words or lines slightly out loud, sometimes like a murmur, and other times almost like a buzz or drone that goes on in the background. Rather than being distracting, it's an authentic, wonderful sound that shows that the congregation is participating and keeping up with the pace of the service. They're doing something called *davening,* a Yiddish word for praying. Like many other Yiddish terms, its usage means so much more than just the simple definition. If you're *davening* a service, you really know what you're doing.

Similarly, Jews who are *davening* are not standing still. They may be rocking slightly back and forth, referred to by another wonderfully descriptive Yiddish word, *shochling.* There are times in the service where people take a few steps backward and forward, bow, turn side to side, cover their eyes, hold the fringes of the *tallit* (prayer shawl), and even raise themselves up on tiptoes three times. Taken all together, this is the choreography of a routine service.

INSIDER'S TIP!

IF YOU'RE unfamiliar with the service and not a regular attendee at shul, some of these movements may look strange. When I'm in the "zone" and *davening* along, I'll be moving and *shochling* and getting a good Jewish workout. Sometimes I get some looks, especially from the bar mitzvah kid who is standing near me and isn't used to what all that looks like.

You will undoubtedly feel awkward trying to incorporate any of these actions into your own participation. We're used to more structured and seemingly respectful behavior. When the rabbi asks the congregation to "Please rise," your reaction is to stand up and stand quietly and still. But look around at some of the veteran congregants and you'll see what I mean.

This is one of the huge benefits to coming to services before the big day. You will have an opportunity to observe all this choreography and hopefully learn some of it yourself. It's perfectly appropriate to politely imitate what you see around you, unless you're watching some bored guest texting in the back row.

The Music

We haven't even mentioned the most important part of our big musical production: the actual music! Virtually every bit of the service is sung in some way, and much of it will be led by you.

Now, unlike an actual Broadway musical, there are no auditions, no finding the very best voices to play the lead and telling others, "Sorry, maybe next time." Instead, everyone gets to play the lead, regardless of talent and ability. This may be on the top of your worry list. You know that you can read Hebrew OK, and you can figure out what to do for each page, but you think you have a terrible voice and couldn't possibly sing in front of all those people.

Guess what? You might very well have an awful singing voice. Parents love to tell kids that when they were in school a million years ago, their singing was so bad that the chorus teacher told them to just mouth the words. Over many years, I have heard every possible kind of voice, and I can absolutely assure you that no matter how bad you think you are, your singing probably isn't nearly as horrible as you think.

I have parents tell me before lessons start that their kid is "tone deaf" and it's going to be really hard to teach them to chant the service, let alone listen to them. When they tell me this, I put them at ease, just as I'll put you at ease right now: Only *very rarely* have I come across a truly tone deaf student. Everyone else was able to sing, with varying degrees of ability, and have the tune be recognizable and accurate.

There are different kinds of singing that you'll be doing as you star in *Bar Mitzvah: The Musical.* First and easiest is congregational singing, that is, everyone singing the same song together. Depending on your temple and what the service is like, there may be more or less of this kind of singing. Furthermore, you may be accompanied by guitar or piano, which might make things even easier for you. Usually, congregational singing will let you relax a little bit.

During lessons and while you're practicing at home (you *are* practicing, right?), my advice is to spend the least amount of time worrying about congregational singing. Don't get me wrong—you're the "song leader" and you need to know it well enough to sing along with everyone. But realistically, if it's a song that everyone will be singing together, you'll likely have to start the tune, but then the cantor, rabbi, and everyone in the congregation will start singing with you. There's not a lot of pressure on you.

JUST FOR PARENTS

IT **NEVER** ceases to amaze me how many parents routinely announce to me and everyone else that their son or daughter is tone deaf. Please don't tell your kid she's tone deaf or let her believe that she is. All you're doing is reinforcing the erroneous notion that your child can't sing (and if she does, it will be torture for everyone to hear). While this might give you a chuckle, it may very well have a more profound effect on your child, who is likely already extremely self-conscious about singing in public. Of course, it's not your intention, but by repeatedly throwing around the term "tone deaf" you're increasing her fears and damaging an already fragile self-esteem.

Here's an experiment for you:

Have your supposedly tone deaf child (or, of course, you can try it yourself) sing the song "Happy Birthday to You" out loud.

How did it sound?

OK, so maybe it wasn't pretty. No Grammy awards in your future, but that's fine. Did it sound like the song that we all know? Was it something that other people could sing along with if necessary? I'm guessing the answer to these questions is yes.

Part of the problem with singing when there's not a great deal of natural ability is that the actual challenge of learning and then presenting an unfamiliar tune sometimes gets in the way. If you take away that obstacle by singing a 100 percent familiar tune, suddenly your previously tone deaf person can miraculously sing notes.

Being truly tone deaf means that you cannot discern any difference in notes. You're unable to hear or imitate a note going higher or lower. That's actually quite rare. And even in these cases, cantors and other b'nei mitzvah tutors can get your kid to sing just fine (well, you know, almost) by using a bag of tricks and different strategies.

Sure, there are exceptions, and again, this will depend on what your congregation is like. It's possible that the majority of people sitting in the congregation are not familiar with the service at all. In this case, the audience watching your production might not know that they're supposed to sing together and wouldn't even know the melody in the first place. Your congregational tune would turn into a solo!

Fear not. Your rabbi and cantor won't hang you out to dry. A duet or trio is still easier for you than a solo, and I can promise you that if it's a tune that everyone should be singing, you'll have at least another voice or two helping out.

In most cases, though, the bulk of your singing will be solo. This is a big musical after all, and you are the star. During your lessons, you will spend most of your time learning and practicing all the different tunes and melodies.

The good news is that once you start going through the service you will likely notice that many of the tunes repeat over and over. There is often one basic kind of melody, maybe with just a couple of minor differences that get used repeatedly on lots of different pages. Learn it once and you're all set.

Another kind of solo singing will be when you chant the Torah or haftarah. We discussed trope in great detail back in chapter 3. Remember that it will sound a lot different than other things you sing in the service. You will probably spend the most time in your lessons preparing to do this kind of singing.

Costumes

In addition to wearing either a new suit or dress, you may have to add another very important item to your wardrobe on the day of your bar or bat mitzvah—a *tallit*, or prayer shawl.

It's traditional to wear a *tallit* in services because of a commandment that we read in the book of Numbers. We are told to sew fringes, or in Hebrew, *tzitzit*, onto the corners of all of our garments so that we may remember God's commandments. What a strange instruction!

It makes a little more sense if you realize that back in ancient times, people dressed a lot differently than today; one common type of garment was sort of a rectangular tunic. It had a hole in the middle for you to put your head through, and then the garment came down on either side of your

INSIDER'S TIP!

MANY PEOPLE will refer to the prayer shawl as a *tallis* (TAH-lis), which is simply a Yiddish pronunciation of the Hebrew word *tallit* (ta-LEET). Either way is perfectly fine.

What's the plural? You'll get a bunch of different possibilities:

Taleisim (Yiddish)
Tallitot (Hebrew)
Tallises (Yiddish and English mixture)
Tallits (Hebrew and English mixture)

I suppose out of all the choices, I prefer *tallitot* because it reflects the most modern Hebrew usage. You may hear any of the others and they're fine to use.

body. It did indeed have four distinct corners—two in front and two in back. Our job was to tie little fringes on each of the corners.

The fringes would remain visible to you all the time. They would constantly swing around as you moved and went through your day, so it would have been a really effective reminder to you if you wanted to remember something important, like behaving morally and following Jewish law and the commandments.

Today, we observe this ritual in a different way. Rather than sewing fringes on our clothes, we have a ready-made garment available, complete with fringes already sewn on. By putting on the *tallit* during service, we are able to fulfill this commandment.

Like so many other things that I've told you about, it used to be traditional that only boys would wear a *tallit*. Girls never did. It has become much more common for a girl to wear a *tallit* at her bat mitzvah, and similarly, you will likely see a significant number of women in the congregation with one.

To make things just a little more complicated (oh, why can't something just be simple for a change?), the practice of wearing a *tallit* will differ depending on what kind of temple you belong to. If you attend a Conservative synagogue, the bar mitzvah boy and all the guys will almost certainly be wearing one. Fewer girls (maybe half?) wear one.

INSIDER'S TIP!

YOU HAVE undoubtedly seen Orthodox or other religious Jews with what looks like fringes hanging out from under their shirts or suit jackets. These are indeed the same *tzitzit* that we're talking about. Rather than just donning a *tallit* for a synagogue service and then removing it when the service is over, these Jews are observing this commandment in a stricter and more literal way. They are wearing a *tallit katan*—literally, a "small *tallit*." This garment is worn under one's clothes, almost like an undershirt, and is worn all day long. The *tzitzit* can either hang out or be tucked in.

In a Reform congregation, though, it will depend on the specific synagogue's practice. In some, most people do not wear one, although some guests do. In other temples, more worshippers will have one. This will be nothing for you to worry about—your rabbi or cantor will let you know what the custom is at your shul and what your options are.

Another important item that you'll need to wear during services is a *kippah*, which is simply a head covering of some kind. (Older people sometimes refer to this item as a "yarmulke.") Just like we saw with the *tallit*, there are different options and customs.

The most fundamental reason for wearing a kippah is to show respect for God. By putting a covering on your head, you're symbolically expressing that something more important than you and everyone you know exists. It's a statement of humility. I've always found it somewhat ironic that in our culture, removing one's hat indoors or in a classroom is a sign of respect, whereas in Jewish tradition, it's just the opposite.

There are numerous ways in which Jews observe this custom, and as with so many Jewish rituals and traditions, what you and your family will do depends on the customs of your synagogue. In Conservative shuls, all males (even your non-Jewish guests) will be expected to wear a kippah. Sometimes women have to cover their heads as well, either all the time or just when going up on the *bimah*. Reform customs can differ widely; wearing a kippah may be optional for everyone or perhaps not observed at all. Certainly you'll be told what will be expected of you well before your bat mitzvah.

"What, too much?"

There are also lots of different styles of kippot (you already figured out that was the plural). The simplest is probably the black satin kippah, but they look pretty old-fashioned. You will commonly see kippot of various colors, often chosen by the bar mitzvah family in order to coordinate with a specific color scheme. Most of these kippot will also have the bar or bat mitzvah kid's name printed on the inside lining. Because there are always kippot left over from each week's bar mitzvah, kippot of many colors tend to collect inside the temple's "kippah bin" found at the entrance. I love when kids come in the building, reach inside to grab a kippah, and then ask each other, "Who'd you get?"

Some kippot that are suede or crocheted need to be worn with a little clip or bobby pin. (And when your uncle who's completely bald walks in the temple, everyone will be watching to see how he gets the kippah to stay on his head.)

As with the *tallit*, there can be different options for girls. Sometimes a fancy bow that goes with your dress will suffice as a kippah. Otherwise, you might wear a more feminine looking kippah or maybe one of those thin lacy

JUST FOR PARENTS

ASSUMING YOU have to buy a *tallit* for your son or daughter, you have a ton of options, because other than the necessary fringes on the four corners, there are really no other requirements for the *tallit*. This means that it may be almost any color, style, or size.

My advice to you: Keep it simple!

When you start shopping around, whether it's at your synagogue's gift shop, online, or at a Judaica store, you will be inundated with choices. As you start considering what you might want your child to wear, always ask yourself this most important question: Will this be something he can wear at every *other* service?

Often I'll see a kid with a really fancy and colorful *tallit* at his bar mitzvah. Sure, he looks great. But then some time later, probably when he comes to his friend's bar mitzvah, the *tallit* is nowhere to be seen. Why? It's too much. It's over the top. He feels funny wearing it routinely. And the point, of course, is that wearing a *tallit* is just one of the many things that a kid who is bar mitzvah is now required to do. How ironic, then, that because he feels uncomfortable, he may not wear it anymore after the one day.

The same thing applies for a girl. It's common for parents to try matching the color of the *tallit* to the bat mitzvah dress, or to choose something really delicate and fancy. But again, will this be something she'll want to wear tomorrow? If she comes to a *minyan* wearing a T-shirt and jeans, will that beautiful, delicate, and decorated *tallit* look completely out of place?

Another really nice custom is for your son or daughter to receive a hand-me-down *tallit*, perhaps from a grandparent or great-grandparent. While this is very moving, and I love the aspect of Jewish continuity, the same issue as before comes into play. What does the *tallit* look like? If it's a bit tattered or yellowed, will he want to wear it again? You might finesse this dilemma by having him wear this very special heirloom at the bar mitzvah and have another, more modern-looking *tallit* for everyday use.

If you keep in mind that this is the *first* time your child will be wearing this *tallit*, not the *only* time, you'll have a lot more success.

INSIDER'S TIP!

STOP KISSING your kippah!

You've probably seen or done it a million times. When someone drops a kippah on the floor by mistake, he picks it up, gives it a little kiss, and then puts it back on his head.

We generally consider any item with God's name on it to be holy. For instance, when we accidentally drop a *Siddur*, we are supposed to kiss it as a sign of respect, because it contains God's name. Some people, upon entering the shul, might touch the *mezuzah* and then give their fingers a quick kiss. During services, when the Torah is marched around the congregation, it's traditional to touch the Torah with your hand or *tallit* and then give that a kiss. All of these customs serve to demonstrate that we regard certain objects as being out of the ordinary—they are holy and should be treated with special respect.

The kippah is not one of them. It's simply something to cover your head. It's just a hat. If you walked into shul for Hebrew school one afternoon wearing your baseball cap, and it fell off your head, would you kiss your baseball cap before putting it back on? Have you ever seen a woman kiss one of those lacy chapel caps? Imagine if your shul decided to have a Mexican-themed service one morning and everyone was sitting there wearing a sombrero. Would you kiss the sombrero if it fell on the ground?

When you kiss a dropped kippah, you're saying that item is holy, when in fact it's pretty ordinary. I've always felt that kissing a dropped kippah took away from the truly holy items. Do you really mean to put a Torah scroll and a satin head covering in the same category?

head coverings that sort of look like doilies. (They're called "chapel caps." Really.) It's perfectly fine to ask all of your friends "what kind of kippah are you wearing?"

Ad Libbing

When I was in school learning to be a cantor, a very wise teacher of mine used to say, "The best improvisation is a planned one."

Actors rehearse endlessly before appearing in productions, but they know that anything can happen. In addition to forgetting or fumbling lines, other actors can miss their entrances, lights can burn out, cell phones can go off in the audience, and lots of other things can happen that can throw a meticulously planned musical into a bit of confusion.

What do the actors do when that happens? They go on, of course. They may make up a line or two to get back on track, or change their stage movements to adjust for faulty lighting or characters being out of position. Anything can happen on stage.

And so it is in temple too. On top of everything that you have to memorize—all the words, music, movements, entrances, exits, scenes, motivation—you have to be completely prepared for something to go wrong.

At one bar mitzvah, after I took the Torah out of the ark, I handed it to the student to hold so he could stand in front of the congregation and chant the *Shema* and the other lines before marching around the congregation. Since his hands were full, I held the *Siddur* so he could see the words. As he was singing the page, I got distracted and accidentally turned to the next page before he was done. As he was singing, he looked up at me with a very amused expression as if to say, "What in the world are you doing?" I quickly turned back (while whispering "oops, sorry") and after stumbling a little over some words that were no longer in front of him, he continued.

That was a pretty funny, and very *real* moment. Sometimes the best action is unexpected and unscripted. Do you know this student, now grown, loves to tease me about how I messed him up at his bar mitzvah?

The Bottom Line

Obviously a bar mitzvah service is not a lavish musical, and you're not the star, although you will certainly be featured during much of the service. The prayers aren't your lines, the cantor and rabbi are not actors, and your *tallit* isn't a costume. I just wanted to show you a different way you can look at things as you begin to prepare.

If you were suddenly cast in a play as the lead and had the opportunity to see that play as many times as you wanted, I know that you would check it out, and probably more than once. Treat your service the same way. Come to services as many times as you can ahead of time. You'll feel much more comfortable during your own bar or bat mitzvah service if you're familiar with the service at your synagogue.

CHAPTER 8

Revenge of the Bar or Bat Mitzvah Kid

I CAN'T THINK of anything that kids love more than to be really good at something and watch their parents struggle with it.

Parents have lots of different skills and often like to pass them along to their children. That's why you'll often find families where both the parents and kids play the same instrument, or are good at the same sport. And all parents know that there comes a point when their kid surpasses their own level of expertise. It can be a humbling experience to wake up one day and realize your child has become better at something than you ever were.

Learning how to sing the tropes and navigate your way through the *Siddur* is also a skill that parents may know something about. In some cases, though, parents have never learned this material at all and are in awe at what you know and how you're able to sing through the words with seemingly no effort. You can take great pride in being able to perform a difficult task that your parents could never do!

But why stop there? After all, you've been going to lessons for months and having to practice and work and suffer. Why should everyone else in the family get a free pass? There are various "assignments" that you might consider handing out to different family members. It makes your bar mitzvah service more meaningful when you spread the participation around, and you'll get to enjoy watching other people make the effort to master one little thing when you've already learned so much.

The Honors

Let's first take a look at many of the possible honors and other assignments that you and your family will likely be able to distribute at your service. Exactly what you're allowed to hand out will differ somewhat depending on the policies of your temple, but a lot of this is pretty straightforward.

An honor is simply some form of participation that you're asking a relative or friend to do. ("Would you read this prayer at my bat mitzvah?" "Oh, I'd be *honored!*") Some honors require the person to sing something, usually in Hebrew, while other honors might involve an English reading or performing some action, like opening the ark doors or standing with a Torah. Sometimes it's a challenge matching the right people with an appropriate honor.

The Torah Service

Most things that you might invite people to do will revolve around the Torah service. The most important honor associated with the Torah service is called an *aliyah*. In fact, it's so important that you'll be receiving one as well.

The word *aliyah* literally means "going up" because the Torah scroll is such a respected and revered item in the service, that you consider it to be on a higher level than anything else in the room.

In a traditional service, on Shabbat, when you're likely to have your bar mitzvah service, there are seven people called up to the Torah, or put

INSIDER'S TIP!

PEOPLE SOMETIMES use the word *aliyah* as a general term to describe any honor. Parents will consult with me or the rabbi and ask us for help in handing out the *aliyahs*. (The real plural term is *aliyot*.) I think that it's great that they are familiar enough with this Hebrew term to be able to use it freely, but they invariably get confused because when *we* use that word, we're only talking about something very specific.

Opening the ark, for example, is not an *aliyah*. *Aliyah* refers only to getting called up to the Torah.

another way, there are seven *aliyot* handed out. In many synagogues, the congregation will let you "have" a certain number and reserve the rest to honor members of the congregation. This makes a lot of sense, because if your temple has a bar mitzvah just about every week, then that would mean people in the congregation who attend services regularly would almost never receive an *aliyah*.

In addition to bar mitzvah family members and friends, it's traditional to honor other congregants or guests. In a smaller shul, for instance, you might have the same core group of worshippers each week. So if someone new showed up, they would welcome that person by offering him an *aliyah*. It's also traditional for a person to come to services on the *yahrzeit* (the anniversary of the death) of a family member so that they can recite the Kaddish. That person would also traditionally be given an *aliyah* or other honor.

Additionally, there are sometimes rules as to who can get which *aliyah*. Sometimes, the first two *aliyot* are reserved for Jews who are descended from

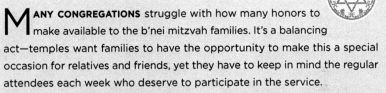

JUST FOR PARENTS

MANY CONGREGATIONS struggle with how many honors to make available to the b'nei mitzvah families. It's a balancing act—temples want families to have the opportunity to make this a special occasion for relatives and friends, yet they have to keep in mind the regular attendees each week who deserve to participate in the service.

Consider the fact that your child's bar mitzvah may not be the only special event taking place in services that week. Perhaps another family is naming a baby, or a congregant has recovered from a serious illness and would like to recite a traditional prayer after getting an *aliyah*. The beauty of the weekly Shabbat service is that it's a venue where the congregation can come together to celebrate special life cycle events. I think b'nei mitzvah services get most of the attention, but there are often other things going on.

If you belong to a synagogue that's smaller, or celebrates just a handful of b'nei mitzvah each year, it's possible that you will get access to every honor. On the other hand, if your congregation is larger, and there's a bar mitzvah many of the weeks each year, it's an extremely reasonable policy to provide you with just some of the available honors.

an ancient priestly class, referred to as a *Kohen* or a *Levi*. It's no accident, by the way, that those happen to be two pretty common Jewish last names. That was one way that this status was preserved throughout the generations. Back when the Temple stood in Jerusalem a couple thousand years ago, these *Kohanim* and *Levi'im* had particular duties and responsibilities, so in some traditional congregations, their descendants are still accorded the respect of the first two *aliyot*.

How do you know if you're a *Kohen* or *Levi*? I always like to joke that if you don't know if you are one, then you're not. The status of *Kohen* or *Levi* has been consistently passed down from parent to child, even among non-observant Jews, who I think still feel a bit of pride deep down for the extra title. The term for a non-*Kohen* or -*Levi* is simply *Yisrael*, which basically refers to miscellaneous Jews—in other words, most of us.

Traditionally, there were additional rules about who could receive which *aliyah*. Shuls would avoid handing out consecutive *aliyot* to a father and son,

INSIDER'S TIP!

MORE FUN with names. Historically, surnames (better known as "last names") are a recent development. People were commonly known by their given first name, and then maybe by their father's name. So many different cultures have remnants of this. Think of surnames like "Robertson" or "Thompson." The prefix "Mac" or "Mc" also means "son of," so we have some guy named Donald to thank for eventually inspiring the guy who named the Golden Arches.

In other cases, it was a person's profession that identified him. That explains surnames like "Taylor" or "Baker," just to name a couple. There are numerous Jewish surnames in Yiddish like this. If you know anyone named "Schneider," it's likely his ancestor was a tailor. The origins of names is a fascinating subject all by itself.

Similarly, Jews would be identified by their special status, so that would explain the surname "Cohen." Other surnames that are common to *Kohanim* are "Katz," "Kagan," or "Cohn." *Levi'im* might be readily identified by names like "Levy," "Levenson," or "Siegel" (which comes from a Hebrew acronym referring to a *Levi*).

or to brothers. (Notice how these were all males; that shows that we're going back in time a bit.) The reason for this has its basis in superstition. People used to think that having a father and son, or two brothers, come up back to back would be what some of your grandparents called a *keinahara*, literally an evil eye. It was supposedly tempting fate by putting so many members of one family on display, like you were just asking for something bad to happen. As you can imagine, I think that's pretty silly. Obviously, at someone's bar mitzvah, it was pretty difficult to juggle all the people receiving *aliyot* so that you didn't have siblings or parents and children in sequence. It's just as well that this practice has fallen out of use, but it's possible that you may come across it.

Not confused enough yet?

When are seven *aliyot* not enough? In some synagogues, they have so many congregants and guests whom they want to honor with *aliyot* that they'll actually add extra ones. (Yes, they can do that and it's kosher.) These extra *aliyot* are called *hosafot*, which means . . . wait for it . . . extra ones. I'm not a big fan of adding *hosafot* because it makes things go on longer, and anyway, where do you stop? Is one extra enough? Why not two, three, or another seven? Theoretically, there's no limit to how many *hosafot* you can add to the Torah reading, but your shul probably has a specific policy on whether to add *hosafot* to the service and, if so, how many.

So your family will get to hand out some number of *aliyot* to relatives and friends. It's a safe bet that any grandparents who are there will be called up, as well as your parents. Although an *aliyah* is an honor given to one individual at a time, it's become very common for couples to be called up, or sometimes groups of three or four at one time.

Anyone who receives an *aliyah* is usually called up to the Torah by his or her Hebrew name, followed by the name their parents, also in Hebrew. So, for example, if your Hebrew name is Shlomo (and if it is, don't tell anyone—just kidding), and let's say your dad's name is Yosef and Mom's is Leah, then you would be called up for your *aliyah* like this:

Ya'amod: Shlomo ben Yosef v'Leah

which loosely translates to:

Hey! Shlomo, son of Yosef and Leah, c'mon down!

Notice how this harkens back to that time when people didn't have last names, but were known by their father's name. So your parents and grandparents, and any other friends and family members that you are honoring with an *aliyah,* need to know their Hebrew names, as well as their parents' Hebrew names (usually just the father's or the mother's is fine if that's all they know). I find it interesting that there are a lot of Jewish people out there with no idea what their Hebrew names are. Sometimes they will bring in a copy of their Jewish wedding certificate for me to examine, because that

INSIDER'S TIP!

Your HEBREW name is so important because it's used at all life cycle events. Shortly after you were born, you were most likely given your Hebrew name. If you're male, that took place at your circumcision (ouch—glad this book is not *Surviving your Circumcision—The Ultimate Insider's Guide*), or, if you're a girl, at a later date, possibly in shul during a baby-naming ceremony.

During your bar mitzvah, you get called up for your very first *aliyah* by your Hebrew name, and then of course, at any service after that. When you get married, your Hebrew name is used in the Jewish wedding ceremony and the *ketubah,* the wedding contract. And you can probably see where this is all leading: At a Jewish funeral, we recite a prayer for the person who died using his Hebrew name, and the Hebrew name is usually inscribed upon the gravestone as well.

Remember that the form of your name that is most often used is this:

Your Hebrew name, son/daughter of Your Father and Mother

There can be some minor exceptions to this. For instance, if you have one parent who is not Jewish, there are a couple different ways to handle this, which will differ based on your rabbi's opinion, so it never hurts to ask.

Finally, some people's Hebrew names are actually Yiddish names. I see this often with parents whose own parents were immigrants to this country. Yiddish names used to be very common in "the old country," but don't really resonate so much anymore. Rabbis and cantors are easily able to hear a Yiddish name and give a close Hebrew equivalent.

will contain their Hebrew names within the text. I have also been asked to look at pictures of gravestones so that I can read the Hebrew names of grandparents or great-grandparents and help in that way. The moral of the story is: Always know your own Hebrew name as well as your parents'.

Each person coming up for an *aliyah* has to sing a short blessing. As I briefly mentioned way back in chapter 1, this is often a real obstacle for a lot of people, but it certainly doesn't need to be. The words are almost always provided, in both Hebrew and transliterated (sounded out) English letters, so that anyone can make their way through the text. But if people are not familiar with the words, they really need to practice. I can't tell you the number of times I have seen well-meaning relatives come up to the Torah and absolutely butcher the words. And why? Did they only hear that morning that they would get an *aliyah*? Didn't they have weeks or even months to do ten minutes of preparation? Many times, the family of the bar or bat mitzvah will be able to hand out photocopies of the blessing to all of their guests who will be receiving an *aliyah*. It's also very easy to find the text and melody online, and even sometimes right on the temple's website.

You, on the other hand, are now the expert. You probably learned these words and this tune very early on, either in your lessons or in Hebrew school one year. Please feel free to nag your parents or older siblings that they need to practice the *aliyah* blessings. And then take great pleasure in watching how stressed out and nervous they get when they have to do one little paragraph when you're busy learning pages and pages of complicated haftarah and prayers.

Reading the Torah

Each time someone gets called up for an *aliyah*, whether it's a member of your family or simply a congregant, some section of the Torah will be read. Back in chapter 3 we talked all about trope symbols and some of the challenges regarding reading the Torah. Remember that in addition to knowing how to sing the trope melodies, the reading usually has to be memorized enough so that the reader can chant right out of the scroll, which is written with that fancy calligraphy.

Still, it's fairly common for families to hand out Torah readings for some relatives or other guests to do. In some cases, you might have someone in your family that you know is able to read the Torah. One of my favorite things is when an older brother or sister reads the Torah at the bar mitzvah—they're using a skill they themselves learned not too long ago. Similarly, often a parent will read the Torah as well, assuming they learned how at some point.

It's really important that anyone in your family who's reading Torah knows what your temple expects. Assuming the Torah is read in the traditional fashion, right from the scroll, your reader is going to be in for a rude surprise when they come up to the *bimah* hoping to just sing the words out of a book.

A lot of cantors have gotten smart about this and require guests they don't know to "audition" before the service. This just means that they want to hear the out-of-town guest sing through the Torah reading first so they can make sure everything is ready.

Again, there you are with months of lessons under your belt and countless melodies and words committed to memory. Maybe you get to watch your older brother or sister struggle with a short Torah reading and become really nervous while you can act like the seasoned professional. All the better if Mom and Dad have to nag them to practice. Feel free to enjoy watching someone else in the house having to worry. You've earned it.

One of the more satisfying moments in kids' b'nei mitzvah services is when the older brother or sister comes up to read the Torah, obviously quite nervous, while the bar mitzvah boy is sitting there secure and confident. I figure, how often do you get to be so much better at something than your older sibling?

Other Honors You Can Let Everyone Else Worry About

There are even more tasks that are usually performed during the Torah service. These include *hagbah*, which means "lifting," and *g'lilah*, meaning "dressing." It's fairly common for a guest or family member to be called up for these during a bar mitzvah service.

Hagbah actually takes some skill, even though it's a non-speaking part. The person who gets this honor is supposed to lift the Torah scroll up by its rounded wooden handles after all the readings are complete, hold it high and turn around so that everyone in the congregation can see inside, and then, while still holding the Torah steady, sit down in the chair which someone else will point out. Depending on the size of the Torah, this honor can require a bit of strength.

Now it's time for *g'lilah*. Every Torah scroll has lots of "accessories." There is a cloth or other type of belt that gets wrapped around the scroll to hold it closed, a cover that goes on top of that, and then very often a bunch of "bling," including silver ornaments and crowns that decorate everything. Someone from the congregation, whether it's the rabbi, cantor, or other helper, will almost always assist the person doing this job.

INSIDER'S TIP!

I HAVE WITNESSED some very scary *hagbah* moments in my many years of being a cantor!

Each Torah scroll is unique. Some scrolls are quite large, and therefore very heavy, while other smaller scrolls are surprisingly light. In addition, because the Torah is an actual scroll and is read in order throughout the Jewish year, depending on when the service takes place, much of the parchment that makes up the Torah could be wrapped around one side so the weight is not balanced. For example, toward the beginning of the Jewish year, from around October through February, most of the scroll will be wrapped around the left side. Later in the summer, the opposite will be true; the bulk of the parchment will be wound around the right-hand side. Either way, unless your bar mitzvah falls midway through the Jewish year, the weight of the Torah scroll will not be evenly balanced between the two handles.

On the Jewish holiday of *Simchat Torah*, when we celebrate coming to the very end of the Torah and then starting over with the first word, the honor of *hagbah* can be particularly challenging. All of the parchment will be wrapped around one side of the scroll while the other side will be completely empty. Combine that with a large and heavy Torah, and you've got yourself a pretty tough job.

When your family decides whom they'd like to honor with *hagbah*, please try to pick someone who's somewhat strong. This isn't the right choice for ailing Aunt Ida who's just getting the hang of her walker.

Opening the ark, either at the beginning of the Torah service or at the end, is probably one of the easiest honors there is. And yet, you guessed it, people still stress out over it.

I have had numerous out-of-town guests come up to me before the service begins, say that they're opening the ark, and ask if they could practice. Now, I'm all about preparation. But I just can't help but feel that people are overthinking this one a bit. Unless your synagogue's ark is something that might appear in the latest *Transformers* movie, usually opening the ark is as simple as either sliding the doors to the side or pulling them open. Some arks have a curtain inside that needs to be pulled open as well. Again, the rabbi or cantor will let the honoree know exactly what to do.

Readings

Depending on your particular service, there may be some additional readings or other prayers that your family can assign. Most often, these readings are in English, and they may involve prayers on behalf of our country or a hope for peace. They may be read alone, or with everyone in the congregation reading along, or responsively with you and the congregants taking turns.

Sometimes, your synagogue will allow you to choose what readings you'd like your guests to recite. Additionally, parents are often given the opportunity to make a short speech or blessing. After everything that parents have to go through in the weeks and months leading up to the service, giving that short speech in front of everyone is often the one thing that they're most worried about.

If some guests will be doing these honors, it would be nice for them to receive a copy of the readings in advance, if that's possible. Even though most people read English just fine, remember that most people get nervous about being in front of so many people (and by now, you're cool as a cucumber), and they may stumble over unfamiliar words, or even familiar ones. Actually, you wouldn't believe some of the mistakes I've heard. On second thought, definitely get them the readings in advance.

The Bottom Line

Perspective is everything. While you're busy chipping away at this huge amount of material, it's easy to lose sight of how much you're learning and what an impressive amount of progress you're making. But then you get to watch other people come up and be nervous about doing things that you can do easily, like reciting a short blessing in Hebrew, or standing in front of the congregation to read an English paragraph.

The result? You'll feel a lot more confident in your own abilities when you realize just how much you actually know, and that's a great feeling. You can consider yourself the seasoned expert and watch how much *more* nervous everyone else if they have to get up in front of the congregation.

CHAPTER 9

Help! My Parents Are Driving Me Crazy!

A H, NOTHING like a little bar mitzvah to throw your entire lives into utter chaos. It's not like you have anything substantial to worry about, right? You attend a couple lessons, your parents order some food, everyone gets dressed up, and the rest just takes care of itself.

Not!

Life cycle events like this are stressful. Not only does everyone in the family have many things to worry about and stress over, but there are emotional issues as well. What should be a time of celebration and togetherness can very easily turn into a period of fighting, bickering, and tension, both within your immediate family and extended to outside friends and relatives.

The good news? It's completely normal.

The bad news? You get to look forward to it.

Let me offer some perspective to both kids and parents to help everyone JUST. CALM. DOWN!!! (Sorry, I guess the pressure is getting to me too.)

Five Life-Changing Words

Here they are: *Worry about your own thing.*

The absolute biggest mistake that anyone in your family can make is to worry about the wrong thing. Does that mean that there's a *right* thing to get nervous about? Of course. For all the kids reading this, your job is to prepare for your service, Torah reading, and haftarah by getting through your lessons, practicing, and eventually stepping up onto the *bimah* and standing in front of everyone. If I were you, I'd worry about that. That sounds like a pretty big job.

Along the way, you have to keep track of your materials, budget your time for practicing, deal with your cantor or other bar mitzvah teacher, as well as juggle your non–bar mitzvah responsibilities like homework and other extracurricular activities. For the average thirteen-year-old, that's a substantial burden to carry.

For parents, well, you've got to worry about everything else, don't you? Just to name a few, you've got invitations, caterers, handing out honors, clothes shopping, as well as the very significant additional stress of *paying for it all.* I'm sure that at times you just feel like running away from the whole thing.

The problem arises when kids and parents also take on each other's burdens.

I'll help you sort out who should worry about what. We'll create two corners, one for the kids and one for their parents. Everyone make your way to your own corner.

The Kids' Corner

Let's decide right from the beginning that you will be in complete charge of *anything* having to do with practicing and preparation.

It's not fair having to get your parents involved in your homework. And what could they do about it anyway? No matter what path you take to get there, you'll be the one who has to sing all this material. So even if you procrastinate, fuss, cry, avoid, fight, and make a complete misery of the entire experience, what good will it do you?

I will talk much more about this in the next chapter, but the more responsibility you can take with this stuff the better.

The Parents' Corner

By the same token, avoid the urge to get involved in your child's preparation. I have had students who relied on their parents to remember everything, and the parents just went along with it, not realizing that they were needlessly adding to their own list of important things to do.

Once in a while, I'll ask the student to bring something in for the next lesson. It could be a CD that I handed out, perhaps because I want to double check something that I recorded on a track. Maybe it's a sheet or handout about the tropes that the student took out of the folder and left at home. So I might say, "Could you make sure to bring that with you next week?" A very simple and straightforward request.

Occasionally the student will turn to his mother (who just came in because it's the end of the lesson and they're ready to go home) and say, "I have to bring my CD next week. Can you remember that for me?" And then . . . this is the best part . . . the mother takes out her little to-do list and jots down that the kid should have his CD next week.

Wow. Here's a thirteen-year-old with his own personal assistant.

There's so much wrong with that scenario I can't even hope to cover it all. But the worst thing is that the child has taken a very simple chore and dumped it onto the parent, who now has *one more thing* to remember.

Parents, don't do it. The proper response should be, "No, *you* remember to bring in your CD next week. That's your job. My job is to get you to lessons."

Teaching to the Test

A lot of potential stress can result from exactly how you and your parents are envisioning the service.

Think about all those annoying standardized tests that you have to take during various grades. Your teachers are required to cover certain material that's on these tests, and that means that they sometimes have to suspend their regularly scheduled lesson plans in order to do that. This is sometimes referred to as "teaching to the test." (And teachers generally hate doing it.) Sometimes it feels as if what is most important is not the actual learning but rather how the student performs on the test. During testing week, it's common for schools to send notes home reminding parents to make sure their kids get a good night's sleep, and eat a nutritious breakfast (I guess candy and chips are fine the rest of the year). Some kids get pretty stressed out knowing that they'll be taking these standardized tests, and their scores will affect what classes they'll be able to take in future years. All the preparation leading up to the testing, and the emphasis that school puts on being ready, can add a lot of pressure to a student's life.

If you think about it, there are similarities between preparing for a standardized test and preparing for your bar mitzvah. If you imagine that your bar mitzvah service is your big "test," then all your lessons consist of teaching to that test. That takes most of the focus off the learning and places most of the emphasis on a single event, the two or three hours that your service will last.

Are you thinking about anything *after* your bar mitzvah? Unfortunately, just like a school's standardized test, once your bar or bat mitzvah is over, and you've gotten through it, you'll probably think that you don't need to worry about it anymore. Whew, glad that's over. Now I can get on with my life. Certainly, I think it's pretty common for both kids and parents to view the bar mitzvah this way.

Unfortunately, if you're thinking this way, your bar mitzvah service becomes a very pressure-filled two-hour period. If you get caught in the trap of considering your bar mitzvah as nothing more than an intense two-hour test, it seems like there's no room for any error or deviation from the plan. Everything must go like clockwork or it'll be a disaster. You will have done poorly on the "test" and there's no second chance.

And you wonder why everyone in the family is stressed out.

Parents: Resist Micromanaging the Service

Don't think of the bar mitzvah as *the* service, but rather as the *first* service that you'll be participating in. I know that's difficult. First, you have all your relatives and friends and guests who will be at this one service. It's not like they'll see you up there any other week. Second, realistically, you're probably not used to attending services on a regular basis.

However, all the skills that you're learning, whether it's how to lead a service or how to use the tropes to sing the Torah, don't expire on the day of your bar mitzvah. Those are things that we really want you to do many times in the future.

Frequently, parents and kids begin to view the bar mitzvah less as a service at which we're honoring a freshly minted adult member of the community, and more as a pageant. Let's parade the kid up there and show everyone we know how talented and wonderful she is. Yes, I know that I just went through a long explanation in chapter 7 comparing a bar mitzvah service to a big Broadway musical, but I was careful to explain that the reason was simply to make some tasks that you have to remember a little easier to understand. The problem arises when some families really do treat the service like a production.

It's hard not to! You are being pummeled from every direction with information about party planning, caterers, reception halls, suits, dresses, rehearsals, and countless other details that are all trying to convince you that this is in fact a huge show starring the bar mitzvah student. It can be extremely difficult to swim against that particular stream.

Remember, this is your *first* service as a Jewish adult. Hopefully, the first of many.

Sometimes, a parent will tell me, at the beginning of bar mitzvah lessons, "I want my child to do all the Torah readings."

What I'd really like to respond with is "Why?"

Lessons and services work differently depending on what temple you belong to. A fairly typical setup is to have the student begin learning the normal amount of material. This might include chanting the haftarah (which by itself will likely take months of work), learning a Torah reading, and some parts of the service. For many kids, that's plenty! That'll keep us busy for pretty much the entire time. Some students have difficulty getting through the normal amount (even if they're practicing regularly and making a real effort), so we modify our expectations a bit and may reduce the amount of material. Depending on the customs in your temple, your cantor may have some flexibility with the length of the Torah reading or haftarah. There's nothing wrong with this realistic approach. Still other kids move really fast. They show a remarkable aptitude for the material and we fly through it, meaning that there's some time left to add more stuff.

That's why if you attend b'nei mitzvah services regularly (and if you don't yet, you will!), you'll see all the kids at your temple do mostly the same thing week after week, but some kids will do a little less, and others might end up leading or singing a significant amount more. For instance, if there are Torah readings that can be assigned, a bar mitzvah kid might have learned one, two, three, or even all seven of them.

Soon, it becomes a subtle competition. Who wants to be the kid who couldn't learn a Torah reading? On the other hand, imagine the pride of the parents who get to watch their daughter read every word of Torah.

Try really hard to avoid this thinking.

Sure, it looks impressive when a kid is able to learn all the Torah readings. I love when I have a student like that. That definitely makes my job easier, both throughout lessons and then during the service. And frankly, it makes me look good in front of the congregation. When members of the congregation who happen to be in the service that week get to see a really talented student, there's a perception that the professionals that they hired and pay every week are really doing a great job.

But take the other side of that. At times we have a bar mitzvah student who struggles with the learning. Perhaps there's a learning disability or other important issue involved. Still, each week, that student practices diligently, works *very hard* at decoding and learning the prayers, and makes progress consistently. In my opinion, that's a dream student.

Flash forward to the bar mitzvah service. Maybe we worked so hard and successfully only on certain tasks, so that this student will not read the Torah, won't lead some pages of the prayer book, and might even struggle a bit through an abbreviated haftarah. Parents, if you're part of the "my child needs to do everything" school of thought, then, by definition, this bar mitzvah kid did a lousy job and didn't accomplish much.

Think back to chapter 7 for a minute, and pretend once again that this isn't a service but rather a big staged production. Each week, you see the same show with a different star. One week, the "star" doesn't do all of his lines! He has trouble reciting other parts of the script. Boooo! The bad reviews start pouring in.

Clearly, this is not how we should be looking at the bar mitzvah service.

Back to my micromanaging parent. What do you think would happen if I responded to "I want my child to do all the Torah readings" by explaining that learning every *aliyah* of Torah is very difficult and unlikely, so instead, how about if we set a date a month or so after the bar mitzvah, and I'll help him learn another Torah reading to do at that service?

(Listen to the coyotes howling in the distance.)

That's not what the parent was looking for at all, was it? But that nicely illustrates my goal, and what should be *your* goal in looking at this as just the first service you'll be involved in.

What's the point of adding a very significant amount of pressure by insisting at the outset that a student *must* learn all the Torah readings? Is it so the child can learn how to read the Torah, or so the child can knock the socks off of every relative and friend who attends?

I'm using the Torah reading as one example. The bottom line is that by micromanaging in this way, you're creating needless opportunities to get stressed out. And the added pressure on the kid is incredible.

Some students have been brought to tears because they were convinced that if they didn't learn more and do it faster, they'd get in trouble at home, even though I was thrilled with their progress. (And alas, they were probably right.)

Another reason parents fall into the trap of micromanaging things is that they lose sight of the fact that there are services every week. Here is yet another reason why it's important that you attend services more often, at least during the year surrounding the bar mitzvah. Because there's so much preparation and hype, it's easy to start thinking that this one service exists to feature your child. If that's how you view the service, you might start to get upset if your daughter is not allowed to lead every bit of services, if some honors are reserved for Jewish friends and relatives only, or if perhaps there is another happy occasion taking place that morning as well, such as a baby naming or an *aufruf* (honoring a soon-to-be married couple), that you think will take away from the attention focused on the bat mitzvah kid.

Put yourself in the place of a regular congregant who attends every Shabbat, likes to sit in the same place, and enjoys *davening* and seeing his friends and fellow temple members. How might you feel if some family, which you've never seen before, took over the whole service, tried to assign

INSIDER'S TIP!

THERE ARE, in fact, some shuls where they only have a service when there's a bar mitzvah going on. This could be because the membership itself is small, so that they don't regularly have enough people to maintain a service unless there's something going on. Perhaps the service is taking place not on a busy Shabbat morning but rather on a less common day, such as a Monday morning. In these cases, you or your parents might have some more freedom to make some changes or modifications to the service.

where everyone was going to sit and what parts of the prayer book the cantor would be "allowed" to lead, and generally tried to orchestrate the entire thing from start to finish?

Instead, what if you and your family were also regular congregants? Everyone else who attended regularly would already know you. Your child would be "one of their own," getting to lead services. You would already know how services go and what they look like, so you wouldn't feel the need to adjust things the way you think they should be.

Kids: Resist the Household Stress

During the time leading up to the bar mitzvah, and especially as you get closer to the date, there's a ton of what I call background stress in your house. You can feel it. Everyone is on edge, tempers are short, and you get the feeling that your parents are on the verge of a nervous breakdown.

On the morning of the bar mitzvah, the family will arrive at temple (so far so good) and you can tell, just by looking at their faces and the way they walk in, that things haven't been pretty in that house before they got here. Sure enough, the bar mitzvah boy, who is otherwise well prepared and completely ready to go, will lose it. Total meltdown. Who can deal with that kind of stress? Now I have to talk down a sobbing child in my office and get him ready to start the service.

What is this poor kid upset about? Is it chanting page 136 correctly? Remembering a tough trope on the last page of haftarah? Not really—as I said, he already knows all that stuff cold. Instead, he has made himself crazy by reacting to the high level of tension in his house. The parents have probably been running around like crazy since 6:00 a.m. and bickering with each other and everyone else at home. (This is a good time for younger brothers and sisters to *stay far away*.)

It's possible that Mom and Dad are nervous about certain relatives arriving in time or the health condition of older family members, or they're upset because it decided to snow or pour that morning. These are all reasonable things to be upset about (although notice that each example is something that no one can do anything about anyway), but no bar mitzvah kid should have to shoulder those burdens as well. It's unfair for parents to involve their kids in all these outside concerns and worries.

You Are Not in Control

That is to say, not in control about certain things. There is nothing like a huge family celebration to bring out the feuding relatives, over-involved in-laws, and perhaps some sibling rivalry thrown in for good measure. You can certainly help decide what style dress or suit you're going to wear. You cannot make your cousins get along and sit happily next to each other at the same table. And yet I have seen families get caught in the middle of fighting family members many times, needlessly adding stress to both the parents and kids.

There are two major areas where you'll likely have to involve family members: your celebration and handing out many of the honors in the service (see chapter 8). The main idea of this chapter isn't conflict resolution and finding ways for all your relatives to miraculously get along. Rather, it's to show how stress, anxiety, and pressure are *contagious*. It gets passed around the family, so that now you've got a thirteen-year-old kid finding it hard to sleep at night because he knows that Aunt Rose won't sit anywhere near cousin Marvin because of the chopped liver incident of 1975. (And we all know that Marvin was at fault, but he'll never admit it. That Aunt Rose is a saint.)

What You Can Do

Like I said before, you're in charge of anything having to do with practicing, preparing, and keeping track of your materials.

Picture the following scenario:

The bar mitzvah family has arrived at shul, but just before the service begins, the bar mitzvah boy realizes that he left his folder at home. Now someone has to run home and get it. (It's usually Dad who makes the trip; I'm not sure why.)

Dad says, "OK, I'll run home and get it. What does it look like?"

"It's the blue folder with a sticker on it." (Kids always put stickers or doodles on their folders.)

"And where is it?"

"It's on my bed."

Do you know that this happens *all the time*?

"I forgot my suit!"

While you can't do anything about the weather, relatives running late, or your baby sister's last-minute decision to throw a tantrum, you can be sure to bring everything you need to shul. Spare your poor parents the panicked dash home to retrieve something you left behind. Get everything ready to go *the night before.*

Another common source of stress is when everyone is running late. And for some reason, maybe due to some weird quirk in the time/space continuum, it never fails that the family that lives right down the street from the synagogue walks in with a scant two minutes to go before the service starts, whereas the families who live further away seem to get there in plenty of time.

You cannot physically make people in your house move faster. However, *you* can make sure that *you're* ready. Don't tell your mother to wake you up at a certain time. Just set your alarm and get up. Be the first one dressed and ready to go.

No one will get mad and yell at you if you're sitting on the couch completely ready and waiting for everyone.

If you've got to deal with makeup and hair and all that stuff that I simply don't understand anything about (I have two sons, thank you very much), the same thing applies. Be up and ready to go. Maybe the hair lady will be late to the house, but if so, at least you won't be the one to make your family late.

My Own Troubleshooting Guide

When you buy an appliance or electronic item, the manual (which no one reads) usually has a troubleshooting guide in the back. You can look up what's not working properly and the manual will give you a solution. Often, they're pretty hilarious. Here's an example:

> *Problem: Appliance will not operate.*
> *Solution: Be sure appliance is plugged in and turned on.*

So here is my own guide to solving, and even better, altogether avoiding common problems and sources of stress that might arise in the months leading up to the bar or bat mitzvah. These are typical situations that parents and kids are likely to come across.

Parent Problem #1: My child is simply not practicing, no matter what I do!

Solution: Stop doing anything. It's your kid's homework. If she doesn't do it, then she won't be prepared adequately for her service. She's the one who will have to bear the consequences of standing on the *bimah* and not doing as well as she could have. Most likely she is quite motivated to sound good in front of her friends, so one way or the other, she'll probably get the work done. But the bottom line is that you cannot step inside of her body and physically force her to sing or prepare a certain way.

Kid Problem #1: My parents keep nagging me to practice all the time!

Solution: So practice. They can't nag you if you're doing it. Otherwise, just tell them in a very nice and respectful way that you're taking it seriously and you've got it under control.

**Parent Problem #2: I've got eight million things to take care of!
A ton of details for the party, travel arrangements for out-of-town
guests, clothes shopping, on and on.**

Solution: I can't help you with all those chores, and you do have a lot to do.
However, make sure that you're only doing stuff that *you* need to do. Are
you overly involved in your kid's lessons or preparation? That's energy that
you don't need to expend. Look at it this way: Would you put your thirteen-
year-old in charge of making hotel reservations for your uncle and aunt
from Cleveland? Right. So why would you assume control of keeping track
of his progress and making sure that he has everything?

**Kid Problem #2: My little brother or sister is bugging me all
the time!**

Solution: This one is so easy, it's criminal. If I had to guess, I'd say that whenever you and your younger sibling argue or get in a fight, you're the one who
gets yelled at more often. Somehow, it becomes your fault. "You're older.
You should know better." It's scary how gifted annoying little brothers and
sisters are at getting older siblings in trouble.

But you're armed with a secret, powerful weapon: your bar mitzvah
materials. Next time little Tommy comes in to make your life miserable,
before you start fighting and call for Mom and Dad, make sure that you're
sitting at your desk or other usual working location, and open your folder
in front of you. When your parents come in to yell at you, they'll see you
trying to practice and your little sibling standing there, obviously distracting you. You might as well be wearing a bullet-proof vest. They can't touch
you. Game over.

**Parent Problem #3: There are too many people to honor,
and not enough honors to hand out in the service.**

Solution: Except people who have particularly small families, almost everyone has this problem. You can get a little creative with certain honors. For
instance, some temples will let you double up on people coming up to open
the ark or do an *aliyah*. Just be prepared for the fact that *someone* is likely to
be upset no matter what you do. It's a life cycle event fact of life. You can't
please everyone.

Just keep your eye on the big picture. It's a service to commemorate the fact that your child is now of a certain age. It's not a pageant in which to parade every family member, friend, neighbor, co-worker, or day care teacher who has ever been involved in your life.

Kid Problem #3: I can't get my CD to work properly.

Solution: Be sure appliance is plugged in and turned on.

The Bottom Line

If I told you that you could get through your bar mitzvah, from your first lesson through the end of the service, without any stress, arguing, crying, bickering, whining, or fighting, I'd be lying. Events such as these disrupt your well-honed routine.

The trick is not to waste your energy on things that are out of your control or that other people should be worrying about. You could lose sleep because the torrential rain that is forecast for Saturday afternoon will be a major inconvenience for everyone attending your party, but since you can't do anything about it, why not just run through your haftarah one more time?

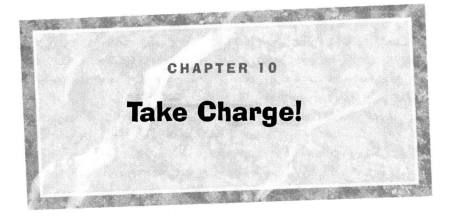

Take Charge!

JUST **REMEMBER,** this is *your* bar mitzvah.

Back in chapter 2, I told you that all your hard work preparing for your service was actually one of the main points of becoming bar mitzvah. It can be a model for how you view and overcome all the future hurdles that you'll face.

In other words, it's all about taking responsibility.

That's a word that keeps on coming up, doesn't it? When you become bar mitzvah, you're told repeatedly that you are now *responsible* for keeping the commandments and performing the rituals. It seems like your bar mitzvah day is the beginning of when you take real *responsibility* for things.

I would disagree!

I think your job is to be responsible way before then. Like as soon as you begin lessons.

Passive Versus Active

Here is how things typically go: At some point months and months before your bat mitzvah date, your parent will contact the temple and ask about bat mitzvah lessons, when they start, how many months they'll last, and other details. They'll eventually schedule a time slot for you and get started.

Throughout the course of lessons, sometimes you won't practice as much as you should (imagine that!), so your cantor or tutor contacts your parent to let them know, probably saying something like, "You need to get your daughter to practice more." To which your parent will probably respond, "I remind her about it all the time."

Another common scenario is when your mother calls the temple and tells your cantor or tutor that you had a really busy week and just weren't able to practice enough, and she either asks to cancel this week or asks your teacher to go easy on you because you're nervous he'll be mad.

Wow, that sure makes your job pretty easy, doesn't it? You don't really have to do anything and Mom and Dad take care of the whole thing. Sweet.

Let's try an alternate reality. How about if it happens this way:

At some point months and months before your date, *you* call your cantor up, or wait until you see him in temple sometime when you're there for services or Hebrew school, and ask when *your* lessons start. Of course, you'll probably have to involve your parents in scheduling lessons, unless you're really precocious and already have your driver's license.

Sometimes during lessons, your cantor might feel that you're not progressing quite as fast as he'd like, or that you could be practicing a lot more, and he tells you this. Together, you two agree and you decide that you'll spend at least a little more time practicing.

Still, there may be some weeks when you'll fall behind everything, and you know the lesson isn't going to go as well as you'd like. When you sit down in the cantor's office, you discuss this with him, and continue with the lesson. You know you should have made more progress, and so does your cantor, but at least you're going over the material.

This second version of events reminds me of the old Peanuts comic strip—the only characters were the kids, and all the action revolved around them. There was never an adult to be seen. Most of the time, I would like bar mitzvah lessons to work much the same way.

I realize that not all teachers and cantors are created equal. Some are not the "warm and fuzzy" type. Some are *scary*. There are kids reading this now who in a million years couldn't imagine sending an email to the cantor or telling him in person, "Sorry, I didn't practice this week."

Try it anyway.

Otherwise you become a passive participant in the whole process. Things just happen around you, and happen *to* you. And you go along with everything and show up where you're told you need to be. You've become a spectator in the conversation between your parents and your cantor.

I think that two of the most irritating and overused words of the twenty-first century are "empowered" and "ownership," and yet I can't think of two better terms for what I'm telling you. You have to own *your* bar mitzvah, and empower *yourself* because it is the beginning of how you'll view yourself and your character. If your mother runs interference for you all along the way and smoothes things over with the cantor when you're afraid you didn't practice enough, how will you look back on this challenge after it's over? You might have gotten through it, but how much did you really accomplish?

This is all starting to sound like a really bad self-help seminar, so let's look at some very concrete examples of how you can take charge. These are all based on frequent and common situations I've experienced with students and parents over the years.

Scenario 1

You have a lesson every Monday. Now it's Tuesday, and since we just had a lesson yesterday, your mother tells you to practice. You finally go to your desk to get your folders, but you can't find them. They're not in your school bag or anywhere else in sight. Mom and Dad haven't seen them either. The following Monday you come to your lesson and say to me, "I didn't practice because I couldn't find my folders. I think they're lost."

How might you have handled this problem better? To me, the main issue isn't that you misplaced your folders, but rather that you lost an entire week of practicing. If you figured out that you couldn't find your stuff on Tuesday, why did you wait until Monday to do anything about it?

One possible solution would have been for your mother to call me and tell me you lost your materials (let's blame it on the cleaning woman again) and ask me to make another set. Sure, no problem, but unless you come pick them up soon, you're still going to go days without practicing.

I have a better alternative. How about if *you* email me (which doesn't seem as intimidating as talking on the phone), and simply tell me that you can't find your folders, say you're really sorry, ask me nicely to make you new ones, and ask when can you pick them up?

That's pretty simple. You had a problem and you took steps to solve it.

If you lost an important notebook for school, would your parents call your teacher for you, or is it something you would have to deal with? Studying and preparing for your bar mitzvah is no different.

Scenario 2

The week went by and you just didn't practice. Now you're worked up and nervous because you know that you're not prepared for today's lesson. You beg your mother to cancel the lesson, and maybe for a little added effect you cry. Mom calls me and either honestly tells me that you're a complete basket case or fibs a little and says that you're not feeling well today. In any event, we'll have to miss this week's lesson.

Let's figure out a better ending. I completely understand that there will be times when you have a bad practicing week. Even if it's due to sheer laziness, I know we're going to have those weeks. But think what a bold statement you would make if you called or emailed me directly and said outright, "Cantor, I'm really sorry but I didn't even open the book once this week. Do you still want me to come in for a lesson?"

I would be thrilled to receive a question like that from you. Here's a kid who's taking charge, realized he got a little off track, and would like to know what his options are. My response would be to say absolutely come in for your lesson. There are a lot of things we can review and go over, and then you can make sure to have a good week of practicing. In this way, we dealt with your progress directly between the two of us, and came up with a good solution.

It's all about passive versus active. Passive means everything happens *to* you. Active means *you* make it happen.

Scenario 3

I get a call from a mother that her son came home from his lesson last time in tears! He's overwhelmed, he's a complete wreck, he doesn't think he's going to be able to learn everything, and she asks whether it's possible to cut back on some of the material.

Often, this is news to me. I can see very well when a student is approaching a meltdown and can react accordingly. Sometimes, though, I speak with a parent and am mystified.

Next week, my student comes back for his lesson and I immediately act to put him at ease: I understand you were really upset last time, I say, and let's see what we can do about it. At this point, he looks at me questioningly and says, "No, I'm OK. I just wasn't completely getting what you were explaining last time."

Whoa. How can two versions of the same event be so completely different?

My student probably did leave the previous lesson somewhat frustrated and got in the car either subdued or a little upset. Yes, some of the stuff might have gone over his head. Or he was just tired that afternoon and couldn't get his brain in gear. Or he was distracted or bothered about something unrelated that happened that day in school. His mother asked what was wrong and then proceeded to get the student all worked up because it looked like he wasn't understanding any of the material, and I wasn't explaining it well enough, and he's got to practice, and on and on and on.

Finally her son reached critical mass and melted down.

Here is an example of a well-meaning, concerned parent assuming all responsibility for the bar mitzvah student's progress. The kid becomes completely passive and lets the grownups deal with each other.

Instead, Mom might have asked her son if he told me during the lesson that he wasn't getting it. Or even what I thought about how things went that afternoon. She could have suggested that when they got home, he could email me and say he didn't understand the last things we talked about, and ask if I could I explain it again better. Wow, how I would love to get an email like that.

That puts the student in control.

I Speak Lessonese

In addition to English and Hebrew, I've become proficient in another language that I get to use on many occasions. It's called Lessonese, because it's spoken almost only during bar mitzvah lessons. I'm happy to share some common phrases in Lessonese and provide the English translations.

My question: "How is this page coming along?"
Response in Lessonese: "I had a lot of trouble with it."
English translation: "I didn't practice it at all."

If we're working on a page or section of the haftarah and I tell you to practice it or prepare it for next lesson, what I really want to see is some progress. Put another way, come in next week knowing more than you did this week. How much more is up to you. If I told you to learn eight sentences of your haftarah, and the following week you could sing through three or four sentences really well but weren't able to keep going, I would be happy with that. You practiced and you learned something. Nice job.

The problem with speaking in Lessonese is that you become passive. It would even be better to just say you didn't look at it during the past week, but you're going to sing it now anyway just to see what you remember from last week. That's an active approach.

My question: "Did you practice this week?"

OK, stop. I mean, how complicated can this be? This is pretty much a yes or no answer. Yes, I practiced. No, I didn't practice. But remember, Lessonese is a very complex language, and is able to take any simple concept and express it in the most passive way. So instead of just answering my question, you respond in Lessonese:

"A little. I was really busy this week."

You don't even need a Lessonese-to-English dictionary for this one, do you? But I'll be helpful and provide you with the official translation anyway:

"No, I did not practice at all this week."

Lessonese is such a complex language that there are many possible responses to the same question. For instance, another reply to "Did you practice this week?" could be:

"I just worked on the reading."

INSIDER'S TIP!

KNOW YOU'RE busy! Students and families have more going on during a regular week than adults ever did when they were kids. In addition to school and your considerable homework and assignments, you have sports, music, dancing, drama, and any other activities that I can think of. So when you tell me that you were really busy this week, I completely and totally believe you. But when you tell me that you were really busy this week and didn't get a chance to practice, I think that's silly.

Here's why: If practicing your haftarah were something that you really liked to do, I bet you a million dollars* you would have not only practiced but also found a lot of time to do it. I would guess that during your really busy week (and remember, I'm not doubting how busy you were) you also found time to talk to and text your friends, watch TV, check Facebook, play your Xbox, listen to music, and do all of your other favorite things.

Also, think back to what I told you in chapter 7. Even sitting down and practicing for maybe ten or fifteen minutes can work for you, assuming you do that on a regular basis. Now try this again. Are you *really* trying to tell me that it was impossible to find *ten minutes* during your day to do some practicing?

---

* Money not actually to be awarded. Offer void in all fifty states and every country on the planet.

I think you're beginning to figure out that every sentence in Lessonese actually translates to "I didn't practice at all this week." That's why it's such a passive way to express yourself. You try every which way to twist and distort and disguise the fact that you simply did not practice.

The active alternative would be to skip right to the English statement and say to me, "I didn't practice." That's a perfectly legitimate thing to say, because it then leads us to have a constructive and positive conversation.

Other than just being kind of lazy, there are actually some realistic situations that I could envision which would get in your way. Whether it's a time management problem, a little brother who won't leave you alone, a serious family situation, or being so mystified by the material that you can't take the first step of even opening the book, I can help you come up with solutions and strategies.

Notice how this is something that we can take care of between the two of us. No parent needs to be involved. This is you taking charge of the process.

There are several main reasons why it's so important for you to take charge and leave your parents out of it as much as possible.

First, your parents have their own things to worry about. They've had to plan whatever celebration you're having, including invitations, food, clothing, and hotel and travel information. And don't forget that they have to *pay* for everything. (Trust me, *they* haven't forgotten!)

Why should they worry about your homework and preparation on top of all that? It's not like they can do anything about it anyway. No matter how much they nag or punish you, you're still the person who has to do the actual practicing.

JUST FOR PARENTS

THIS IS NOT to say there's no place for you throughout bar mitzvah training. If you think of practicing as another homework assignment, I think you'll be better able to see what I've been saying.

Kids deal with homework from school in a bunch of different ways. Some get it done right away and really don't require any supervision at all. Without even asking, you know that it was done. Other kids need to be "encouraged" to get started, and maybe you even have to check their assignment for the day to see what was required and whether it got done.

Either way, your child marches into school each day bearing complete responsibility for the homework. If the work isn't done or is incomplete, that's between your kid and the teacher. Sure, you'll eventually hear about it if it happens all the time, either with a call home or a bad progress report.

Similarly, it's great to check in with your cantor or bar mitzvah teacher on a regular basis and make sure things are going well and on schedule. Typically, you'll get updates along the way even without asking.

Of course, just like in school, there are certainly times when it's appropriate and desirable for you to get actively involved. For instance, if you know your child is practicing and yet leaves every lesson upset, that's a problem that you would definitely need to look into.

**"Rabbi, would you mind standing over there?
You clash with our color scheme."**

Second, remember that I'm big on the whole the-journey-is-the-most-important thing. While you're busy thinking only about the very scary couple hours where you'll be standing up on the *bimah*, I'm watching how you handle your months of lessons. Your real learning and maturing begins a long time before you ever sing a word of Hebrew in public. If performing some songs at the service were really the only thing we cared about, I'd just give you a CD a few months before your date, and say, "Here you go, learn this. See you in a few months." You could certainly memorize it that way, but would you have *learned* anything?

Finally, the most important and obvious reason to take charge is simply because it's your bar mitzvah. When students give me the well-worn excuse, "I was really busy this week because I had a ton of homework, a huge project due, family visiting from out of town, and eight soccer tournaments," my reaction in every case will be "Who cares?" Now, I'll express that in a polite and respectful way, but the idea remains. It doesn't really matter what the excuse is, and the excuse could be perfectly true. When you explain why you didn't practice, it's like you've handed in a paper to a teacher and want her to know why it's not going to deserve an A. It's an extremely passive approach, because you're apparently just hoping that things sort of work out in the end.

Assuming you were truly loaded down with homework and projects during the same time that you were having your lessons, what's the end result? One way or another, you will still be standing on the *bimah* and singing what you need to do on the day of your bar mitzvah. You're not going to make an announcement at your service, "Everyone, thanks for coming. I would have sounded better but I was really busy for the past few months with a ton of homework."

This is why you need to take charge and not be passive. It's all on you. You're the one who will be up there. You can procrastinate, complain, make excuses, cry, negotiate, and avoid as much as you want, but once that important date comes, it's all yours.

INSIDER'S TIP!

LOVE **WHEN** my bar mitzvah student:

- bikes to the temple for lessons.
- arranges lesson times with me by email.
- starts a lesson with the words "I practiced this week!"
- loses the CD I made for him but tells me before the next lesson.
- calls me at shul and says he's home sick from school and won't make his lesson.

Notice how not every item is positive. I love when my student loses his CD? Not really, but I do respect the fact that he took responsibility for it, and immediately tried to solve the problem without *passively* waiting for the next lesson and seeing how I would take care of it.

Each example is another way that a student can be in charge of lessons.

But We're Not Religious
(and Other Things That Keep You Away from Temple)

IT CAN BE really hard for your whole family to adjust to the entire year surrounding your bar mitzvah. In addition to you coming to the synagogue for lessons, everyone in the family will (I hope) be attending services more frequently. You'll be present at other friends' b'nei mitzvah, and for the most part, you'll all be fully immersed in different prayers and rituals.

That's stressful enough on its own. What if you think that your family isn't religious?

First, maybe you're more religious than you think you are.

Religious Versus Observant

Let's get our terms straight.

If you know someone who goes to temple every week, keeps kosher, and doesn't drive on Shabbat, you would probably call that person religious. By the same token, if you don't keep kosher or go to temple that often, you would likely say that your family isn't religious.

People use the word "religious" like that all the time, but I think a better term is "observant." There are Jewish rituals, traditions, and commandments, and some people *observe* them. Therefore, someone who keeps kosher, follows the laws of Shabbat, and attends services could be referred to as an observant Jew. But by defining a person as religious, you're putting value on just the things that he does. Keeps kosher—religious. Doesn't keep kosher—not religious.

Reform Judaism, for instance, doesn't necessarily believe that the traditional Jewish laws are binding on today's Jews. Yet many members of a Reform congregation would consider themselves deeply religious, and would be offended if someone rejected them because they observe Judaism in a different way than a Conservative or Orthodox Jew (and unfortunately, that does happen sometimes).

So when you say you're not religious, you may just be saying that you don't come to services as often as other people. Or that you don't keep kosher and don't observe other Jewish customs. Moreover, you may have the idea in your head that a lot of other members of your temple are way more observant than you and your family are.

That attitude will put you at a disadvantage from day one.

Sometimes I'll bump into a congregant around town and we'll say hi and chat for a while. I have finally learned to stop saying, "Hey, how are you? I haven't seen you in a long time!"

Immediately, the congregant becomes apologetic. "Oh, yeah . . . er . . . I haven't been to temple in a long time I guess, ha ha . . ."

Now that's not what I meant at all. That person thought I was making a judgment about his synagogue attendance, and felt bad because he didn't think he is as religious as he should be.

So I would say "observant" is a more fitting word to describe how you or your family might keep and maintain certain traditions. "Religious" can refer to how spiritual or connected to Judaism you might feel regardless of which rituals you practice. It's a subtle difference, but an important one. You may in fact be very religious, but just not observe some of the Jewish laws.

Another problem with describing people as religious or not religious is that it quantifies what you do. It also implies that being religious is somehow better than not being religious. Unfortunately, I think Jewish kids and adults are constantly getting this message from rabbis, cantors, and other Jewish professionals.

You should keep kosher!

You need to come to shul more!

Stop driving on Shabbat!

And because you might know some people who do, in fact, adhere to these rituals, you think they're "more Jewish" than you, so why even bother to participate?

There's a traditional metaphor that I've heard many times. It says that Jewish observance is like a ladder. Depending on whatever rituals you happen to observe, you may find yourself on a certain rung of the ladder. Over the course of time, you may do more, and then you'd be at a higher rung. The moral of this metaphor, we're taught, is that it doesn't really matter where you are on the ladder, only that you're climbing.

I think this is the wrong message and a destructive image!

Because what's the unspoken part of that? That's right—if you're heading down the ladder, that's bad. You're not a good Jew. You're going the wrong way.

Up is good. Down is bad.

Observing more Jewish laws makes you a better Jew. Deciding not to observe them means you're a lousy Jew.

No wonder you may feel disconnected from services and temple. This is the subtle or maybe even direct message that some people receive whenever they do set foot in a synagogue.

I say it's time to lose the ladder metaphor.

Instead, picture Judaism as a lavish banquet table, filled with wonderful and interesting dishes and delicacies. They're all for you! You can have whatever you like.

This is a more positive message, in my opinion, and one that's very appropriate for a young person about to become bar mitzvah. This is just the very first, small step that you can take in making decisions about which practices and traditions you'll grasp onto. Over the course of time, you may very well change your mind and observe fewer rituals, or practice them in a different way. Remember, we got rid of the ladder image; it's not "bad" when you do that.

However, the most important thing is that whatever decisions you make should be based on knowledge and education, and that's one reason for your family to come to services. It doesn't make a lot of sense to say, "The rules about keeping kosher are stupid!" if you don't understand those laws, know where they came from, and know why some people think they're important today. But if you study the rules and origins of kashrut (the Jewish dietary laws), you might still not feel like keeping kosher, but you'd be making an educated decision.

To use the banquet metaphor, you're perfectly free to eat or not eat anything that's there. But you can't just look at a dish and say, "Yech! That's gross. I'm not eating that!" You have to try it first to see if you like it.

You actually might like something you didn't think you would.

Things That Get in the Way

Let's pretend that you and your family never come to temple. Oh, maybe a couple times a year, on the High Holidays and perhaps as a guest at someone's bar mitzvah. But other than that, not really.

What are some of the reasons you don't attend more frequently? Here are some possible statements that you think may describe you and your family:

- Services are for religious people, and we're not religious.
- We have nothing against services, but we just don't feel like making the time.
- We don't understand or know anything about what goes on in a service.
- Services are boring and they go on too long.
- No one in our family knows how to read Hebrew.
- Our family doesn't believe in God. So it would be hypocritical to be in services.
- We always say we want to come, but all of our busy schedules constantly get in the way.

Do any of the above statements ring true for you? I thought so. We've all been there. Even rabbis and cantors have times when they would rather do something else or maybe sleep late and not come to services. There's nothing wrong with that; it's human nature.

I'd like to examine some of these typical statements and show you ways around them.

Services Are for Religious People

There is a wonderful passage of *Talmud* that gets into a lengthy and complicated discussion of when to recite the *Shema*. That's pretty typical. Now if I had written the *Talmud* I would have been much more succinct:

The *Shema*? Say it at 8:00 a.m.and 6:00 p.m. Next subject.

Oh, but you know that we Jews like to discuss, analyze, argue, and dissect every single subject. The fun isn't in the answer so much as the way you took to get there.

So instead of heading directly toward answering the question at hand, the *Talmud* gives us a little story about Jews who arrived at synagogue to pray. It was supposedly time for them to recite the *Shema*, but rather than doing that, they postponed their prayers. They didn't do the *Shema* at that time.

Why?

Because they didn't feel ready. They weren't sufficiently prepared mentally and spiritually to pray the words of the *Shema*.

I love this story. Written a couple thousand years ago, this story could describe any of us in the twenty-first century. You might think to yourself, "Who is more religious than the ancient rabbis of the *Talmud*?" Yet even they didn't feel religious enough to pray at certain times.

If you constantly think to yourself that you're not religious enough to go to services, you're assuming that everyone who *does* attend services must be a lot more religious than you. And that's just not true.

Belief in God

I'll just put it right out there: You don't have to believe in God to be a good Jew.

I think what Judaism and our prayers and sacred texts do best is to give you food for thought about what you think God might be. Furthermore, it's understood that people's religious thinking changes all the time.

I know people who grew up very observant but identify themselves as atheists now. Others were raised with no religion at all and have found a real connection to Jewish tradition. Some individuals were brought up in another religion altogether and have made the decision to embrace Judaism through the process of conversion. You can't look at yourself when you're thirteen, or thirty-three, or sixty-three, and assume that's how you're going to think about God or religion or Judaism forever.

But even assuming that at this point in your life you cannot express any belief in God whatsoever, that's perfectly fine. There are so many other reasons to be present at services.

You can feel a connection to other members of the Jewish community, who share a common cultural background.

You might like the songs.

If you like writing or poetry, you can find meaning in some of the beautifully written texts or readings.

One of your friends always goes and you like to sit next to her.

If something bad is going in your life, you can get comfort from others.

If you're celebrating something, you can share the news.

None of these things requires a belief in a divine being, and they're all wonderful reasons to come to shul.

Hypocritical?

A lot of people open the *Siddur*, take a look at some of the prayers, and fail to see any connection to modern life at all. They think the words they read have no modern meaning, and they express belief in some old fashioned, ancient system.

That's true. Some of the prayers do sound like that.

How then, they think, can they sit there and *pray* this stuff when they don't mean any of it? That's just being hypocritical and false.

Not at all.

I have always considered what's written in the prayer book to be a jumping-off point. When you go shopping and pick up some package, it might have a picture of that food on it with the words "serving suggestion." It's saying that when you buy this product, you could use it to prepare the dish in the picture or lots of other ways as well. But they're showing you one thing that they think is a good idea and would be popular.

The *Siddur* works the same way. The prayers that are written there are just "serving suggestions" for worshippers who wouldn't know where to start otherwise. After all, could you imagine coming to services, and when it was time to start there were no books and no one leading? Instead, someone just announced that you were supposed to *pray* for the next couple of hours. Our tradition understands that most people don't work like that, so instead we have a *Siddur,* a prayer book filled with texts and blessings that might get us started on the road to thinking about what we think is important.

You also don't have to agree with everything that's written.

There's one well-known text that I love to teach to my students because I think it very clearly illustrates the fact that even though our thinking changes over the course of time, how people behave always remains constant. It's a classic example of seeing something in the *Siddur* that we just can't agree with and finding out that maybe with a little effort, it might be pretty relevant after all.

The words come from the *Shema,* which might be the very first prayer most Jews learned. This well-known line is followed by three paragraphs, and I want to highlight the second paragraph. It is actually an excerpt from the book of Deuteronomy, after the ancient Israelites had escaped Egypt and wandered in the desert for forty years. They were just about to live in their new land, and had to understand what was expected of them.

I happen to hate the flowery English translations that are common in many *Siddurim.* I feel that they are a barrier to non-Hebrew speakers to really connect with some of the prayers. When the translations themselves require a translation, then that makes it more difficult, doesn't it? So I will give you my own, regular, common English paraphrase of this text:

> [God is speaking to the Israelites.] If you really listen to all the things that I'm telling you to do, and obey all my commandments, then I will give you rain when you should have it, so all your crops will grow and you'll have all the food you need. You'll eat as much as you want! But . . . if you disobey me and turn your back on me, then I'll stop the rain. Your crops won't grow and you won't have anything to harvest, and eventually you'll run out of food. Then you'll die and disappear from the land that I'm about to give you.

Ah, just lovely. No wonder people feel they're not religious enough or they don't want to come to shul. Who wants to read this? Is this the message that rabbis and cantors want to share with the congregation?

God will punish you with death if you don't obey all the commandments. Yeah, I'd stay away too.

So what are our options with this seemingly disturbing text?

We could just recite it anyway. If it's in the *Siddur* then it must be important, right? And because most people don't understand the Hebrew words, and probably don't glance over at the English translations, that's likely the most popular choice.

We could skip it. This is not my favorite choice, but I would approve. It means that you're aware of the meaning of the text, and that you're engaged enough to make a choice of what you're saying in services. Even saying "No, I will not say these words which I completely disagree with!" is a powerful statement and shows that you're thinking and making reasonable decisions about the prayers.

In fact, a lot of people do skip these words. In some less traditional *Siddurim*, particularly those found in Reform congregations, this paragraph doesn't appear at all, for just the reasons that I laid out before. It's a text that just doesn't represent the thinking of modern Jews, who probably don't believe that God rewards those who obey Him but kills those who don't.

A middle road would be to preserve these words in our *Siddur*, but search for another way to understand them. Perhaps, literally, this text seems objectionable, but maybe we can dig deeper.

So let's start digging.

For both kids and parents reading this, here's a question for each of you.

Kids: Why do you do your homework?

Parents: Why do you pay your taxes?

Don't give me any high-level, meaningful answers about society or doing the right thing. You know the answer to these questions. You do those things because if you didn't you'd get in trouble.

Put another way, if somehow homework for kids and taxes for adults were *voluntary*, would you still do them?

Probably not, even though you likely understand at some level that both homework and taxes have some benefit. Sure, you can have lots of opinions as to how much homework a certain teacher assigns or the wasteful ways that government spends our tax money, but deep down you know that these things are necessary.

So if that's true, why can't we depend on people to just do what's right? Do your homework so you benefit your education, and pay your taxes so that our society will be able to maintain all of our necessary infrastructure and system of law and order.

Is it possible that even if people *know* what the right thing to do is, they *still* might make the wrong choice unless there was some punishment hanging over them as a consequence? I think that's what this paragraph of text is telling us. It's not literally saying that if we eat a bacon cheeseburger God will strike us down (although your cholesterol level might do it for Him indirectly) but rather that there are rules and laws that we are supposed to obey and sometimes the motivation to do that comes from outside. There's nothing wrong with that—that's just the way that people are.

That's what I try to have in my mind when I get through this paragraph. You may or may not agree with anything I just said. However, if you completely discard this text, you can't even have the conversation.

The *Siddur* is filled with examples like this. It's not meant to be a flat, unchanging book of old, boring words. It's not hypocritical to recite the prayers if you don't agree with the words. In fact, I think the authors of the prayers *hoped* that future generations would feel strongly enough about the texts to give them new meaning and interpretations.

Also, while you were so busy doing all that thinking and reinterpreting, we actually finished the service and it's time to eat.

Services Are Boring

Yup, sometimes.

Just wanted to see if you were paying attention.

If someone plopped you down in the middle of a symphony hall and the orchestra spent the next hour or so playing a long, complicated work of some composer you had never heard of, I bet you'd be *really* bored.

Why? First, you don't listen to classical music. Second, you don't know anything about the composer. Third, it's all a bunch of notes and you just want it to end so you can go home.

What if, instead, you had studied this particular piece of music in school for a few months beforehand? You learned about the composer and where he lived; maybe there was something kind of interesting about his

JUST FOR PARENTS

ONE MAJOR reason many adults strongly resist coming to services is because of negative experiences they had when they were children. Perhaps your childhood rabbi was stern or unwelcoming, or there was some dispute that you remember.

Was your bar mitzvah an awful experience? Did your Hebrew school teacher make your life miserable? I wish I could be in the room with everyone reading this right now so I could watch all the heads nodding.

In fact, this is such a common phenomenon that there is an amusing Yiddish saying (and every saying sounds amusing in Yiddish):

Az men iz broygez oyf'n khaz'n entfert men nit omeyn?
(If you're angry with the cantor, will you not respond amen?)

In other words, the love/hate relationship between congregant and clergy has been going on a long time. This saying, in that bitingly insightful way that only Yiddish possesses, points out the fact that if there's something about your rabbi or cantor that bothers you, or that you disagree with, so you decide not to come to shul anymore, who are you really punishing? Who suffers?

Jewish life has changed tremendously in the past generation. Rabbis and cantors have a more modern outlook, concentrating on the congregation and trying to fulfill their needs. Kids don't get yelled at in Hebrew school anymore (although a parent might get a call home if needed—ask my mother how I know), and no 157-year-old rabbi with a white beard is standing over your child drilling Hebrew letters and holding a ruler to slap his knuckles if he makes a mistake.

Similarly, services are often a lot more participatory than you may remember. The stereotype of the cantor is the image of some old guy who chants endlessly (somewhat off-key, although all the older members of the congregation always point out that he sure was something back in his prime) and sings things that no one knows and couldn't join along with anyway.

Today, your cantor may use a guitar or other instrument (depending on what kind of shul you're in) and likely sings a great deal of congregational melodies. We don't want you to just sit there! Cantors and rabbis have made great progress in no longer presenting a service *to the* congregation but rather helping congregants feel like they are part of one big group reading and praying and singing together.

If you're avoiding temple because of what you remember from thirty years ago, you're in for a big surprise. Or, as the saying goes, this is not your father's synagogue.

And finally, many adults stay away because they're angry. This might be in response to the death of a loved one or some other tragedy or misfortune. Obviously, volumes have been written on this subject, and I couldn't hope to properly address such a sensitive and difficult topic here. If I could point out just one thing, I would tell you that if you do make the decision to come to services, you'll see many congregants in the same position, and perhaps you'll find some comfort in being around others in the midst of a similar struggle.

childhood or something tragic that happened to him at some point that influenced much of his music. Additionally, you learned some basics about symphonies and movements, and how different instruments can be used to provide various sounds. So while you were sitting there listening, yes, you may have gotten bored at times, but you were able to pick out and recognize some of the things you learned in school.

Also, because you had a basic understanding of the common movements in a symphony, you at least had an idea as to the progress of the piece and how long it might be going on. If these things were true, the performance wouldn't seem quite so endless.

Attending a service can be lot like that.

I have always felt bad for non-Jewish guests at a bar mitzvah. You know the ones—neighbors or your parents' co-workers that you have to invite. Obviously, they'll have a wonderful time at the party, but I wonder how they can sit there in services for so long. They probably have absolutely no idea what's going on around them, and they certainly can't understand any of the Hebrew prayers. They like seeing you up there and are vaguely amazed that you seem to be fluent in some other language. But I bet they feel like the service goes on forever.

You might feel the same way. Just like in my symphony example, learning even a little bit about some of the prayers will make it a much more

"But the invite said 8:00 a.m."

meaningful experience. The more parts of the service that you know and recognize the faster things will seem to go.

I also happen to have my own opinion about the length of services. I agree that sometimes they *do* go on too long. There have been some changes made over the years to a typical Conservative service, for instance, that cut down the duration of the Torah reading, and other ways to abbreviate the service. Still, depending on the congregation, a Saturday morning service might last close to three hours. I don't think that's the best way to attract more people to attend; I think that we should be streamlining services and even looking for more sensible ways to abbreviate.

I think the ideal length for a Shabbat morning service is closer to ninety minutes. And yes, you're all welcome to join my congregation.

Too Busy?

You wake up on a beautiful Saturday morning. The sky is blue and the sun is shining. You don't have school and your parents don't have to go to work. What's everyone going to do on such a gorgeous morning?

Get dressed up in uncomfortable clothes and sit in a dark-paneled sanctuary for a couple of hours listening to a bunch of words in a language you don't understand.

It sure doesn't sound great when I put it like that, does it?

Anyway, you probably have a soccer practice, or this is the only opportunity that Mom and Dad have to work on the lawn, go to the store, or get things done around the house.

Shabbat, the Jewish Sabbath, is supposed to get people away from all that. In today's world, that can be really difficult. In a lot of families, refraining from buying and shopping and practicing and building seems impossible. On the other hand, I have met countless families that have made the effort to come to either Friday night or Saturday morning services and then continue their regular weekday routine afterward. Remember, as in everything I've discussed so far, *it doesn't need to be all or nothing*.

JUST FOR PARENTS

WHY DO SO many things in religion seem to be based on guilt? If you look closely at a lot of Jewish jokes, which often poke fun at stereotypes, we Jews can't do anything without feeling guilty. (And by the way, have you called your mother lately?)

A category of feeling guilty is thinking of all the things you think you *should* be doing, and then feeling bad because you're not. Attending services is often high on the list. You may have every good intention of going more often, but like we've seen, it's very easy for things to get in the way.

Don't come to services because you view it the same way that kids think about cough medicine—something that they know is necessary but is ultimately unpleasant and leaves a bad taste in the mouth. Rather, consider all the positive results of increased service attendance, which don't necessarily have to be about religion or God or spirituality.

During these months, your child is learning all about how to lead a service, chant a haftarah or Torah reading, and basically stand up on the *bimah* and be a part of the congregation. If for no other reason, try to make an effort to come more often so that you can experience a greater part of that.

I've seen the positive effects of regular attendance at services many times. A family that usually does not attend services will show up one week, either Friday night or Saturday morning, and be visibly uncomfortable and out of place. They sort of look around and you can tell just what they're thinking: Where do we sit? What book do we use? Are we dressed right? How long will this last?

Something wonderful happens fairly soon. The next week or so, that feeling of discomfort begins to ease. By now, they know a lot of what to expect. They already have a regular spot where they like to sit, and the kids don't seem as bored, because maybe they have a song or two that they recognize and like.

Suddenly, after just two or three weeks, they're not "too busy" for services anymore but rather have made them a regular and seamless part of the weekend routine. Sure, there are tons of other things to do—they just wait until after services.

It's amazing what you can make time for with just a little effort.

Make a Connection to Just One Thing

OF COURSE, the more ways that you can find meaning throughout your bar mitzvah experience, the better. Indeed, throughout this book, I've made a point of urging you to consider the big picture. What does a bar mitzvah really mean? What should you be thinking about? Where does all this fit in to being Jewish? Things like that.

Now, it's time to look at the small picture. It can be overwhelming to remember countless prayers, trope melodies (for both haftarah and Torah), meanings of text, and the structure of all your services. Then, on top of that, you have the feeling that you're supposed to not only *know* all of that but *appreciate* it and use your knowledge everyday for the rest of your life. That is a tall order for anyone, let alone a thirteen-year-old who probably just can't wait to add up the checks and get back to her blissfully temple-free routine.

So don't create expectations that can't be met. Instead, decide ahead of time that you will look for *one* thing—whether it's a prayer, tune, word, feeling, emotion, or anything else—that means something to you. That will be your bar mitzvah connection. There are numerous opportunities for you to do this, and you don't have to fit into a certain mold, believe in God, feel religious, come regularly to services, or all the things that you think adults want you to do. Making your own personal connection is, by definition, something that is perfect for just *you*.

Start Looking

Think about all the many different things that make up your bar mitzvah preparation and performance. You have lessons, meeting with the cantor, rabbi, or other teachers, being in the temple during the week, learning different prayers, talking about the Torah reading, hearing and then singing various melodies, holding the Torah, preparing a speech, getting dressed up, wearing a *tallit*, planning some kind of community service project, getting CDs or mp3s, practicing, standing up in front of an audience, and that's just the stuff I could think of off the top of my head.

In fact, many of the items I just listed could themselves be broken up into even smaller chunks. Preparing a speech, for example, would involve doing a little reading about the Torah portion for your week, understanding some facts about the events and characters, and figuring out some link with modern life that might be interesting for people to hear.

Or how about wearing a *tallit*? This involves more than just slinging a piece of material over your shoulders. You might learn about the *tzitzit*, the fringes that are tied to the four corners, and where the rather strange commandment to wear fringes came from and why we do it. Then you have to choose a *tallit* to wear. Will you and your family make a trip to a Judaica store to pick one out? Order it online? Will a grandparent buy one for you? Maybe your family will travel to Israel and you'll bring one back from there.

Going even further, if you're a girl who is wearing one, is that something common in your family? In your temple? Does it mean anything significant to you to use a religious article that until fairly recently was almost always reserved for males only? Or maybe the opposite is true: Egalitarian Judaism (that is, when men and women are considered as complete equals in all matters of religion and ritual) is just so commonplace that having a bat mitzvah girl wear a *tallit* doesn't so much as attract a yawn. That might mean something to you as well.

As you can see, once you start thinking about making connections, about finding some aspect of your bar mitzvah that is meaningful to you, it can be hard to stop! Above all else, this is a job for just you. No one else can tell you what *you* should find significant. Furthermore, if you took all of your friends who already had their b'nei mitzvah and went around asking what was the most important or memorable part of the experience, you'd get many different answers.

JUST FOR PARENTS

THIS IS something that you can and should do as well.

Along the way, you will also become at least a little knowledgable about the Torah portion, certain prayers, or texts. You will also have the enjoyment and satisfaction of watching your child get good at something. Even though I'm not a big fan of the "Today I am a man!" school of thought, you can sit back and appreciate that your son or daughter is getting older and can begin to assume more responsibility for their life, whether in religious or other matters. That's why it's pretty common for parents to get a little weepy when they see their kid up there. (And then it happens again when they get the bill from the caterer.)

Parents, here's an example. There are some Torah portions that are really interesting, meaningful, action-packed, well known, and otherwise fun to read and learn about. Who wouldn't like to get the week when we read the Ten Commandments, or the story of Noah and the Flood, or of the Israelites crossing through the Red Sea? They've made movies about all this stuff.

Conversely, there are some other Torah portions that might be considered boooorrrrring (page after page after endless page about instructions, measurements, and dimensions for building the Tabernacle), or gross (leprosy and skin diseases, complete with open and oozing sores), or disturbing (prohibitions against incest and other forbidden and objectionable relationships). In my shul, on a kid's first lesson, I might open up his book, take a look at the Torah portion that he has, and joke, "Uh oh, you got the leprosy one!"

Sometimes, parents want to manipulate things so that their kid gets one of the "good" Torah portions. The savvy ones will take the assigned date they got from the temple, find a Jewish calendar for that year, and figure out which Torah portion we read that week. If they aren't crazy about the content, then they might call up the temple looking for a different date.

On the one hand, I applaud a parent who is knowledgable enough to even ask the question, "What's the Torah reading that week?" and then to know how to look it up, and to even have an opinion about it. Ultimately, however, I think this falls into that micromanaging trap I mentioned back in chapter 9. If you're already getting worked up about the content of the

(Continued)

155

Torah reading some three or so years in the future (since a lot of kids get b'nei mitzvah date assignments that long in advance), then you're already taking on too much.

These lesser-known or sometimes weird Torah portions can often become the most interesting or thought provoking, for both you and your child. You may very well eliminate a golden opportunity for you and your child to find a meaningful connection to the text by attempting to choose the subject that appeals more to *you*. In the process, you will be exposed to lesser-known and even lesser-understood passages of the Torah that may really stimulate your thinking.

You've Been Sentenced to Community Service

Sure, we Hebrew school teachers could envision a time when some of our more difficult students over the years might hear these words spoken to them. But in this case, it's something positive, not a punishment.

Many synagogues have a requirement that all the b'nei mitzvah students must perform some sort of charitable project, community service, or combination of a certain number of hours toward helping others. This is to highlight the *mitzvah* part of bar mitzvah. It's more than merely doing a few good deeds or helping old ladies cross the street. (But if you do, first make sure they *want* to cross the street. Man, those purses *hurt!*) The idea, rather, is to illustrate that being Jewish and responsible to observe its teachings is more than just rattling off a bunch of memorized prayers or even coming to services a certain number of times.

There is a huge body of material within Jewish tradition which requires us to give *tzedakah*, charity, to people in need, both within and outside of our communities. An important phrase that explains this requirement is *tikkun olam*, or literally "fixing the world." Have you ever been told by a teacher to straighten up or clean a classroom so that it looks better than it did when you got there? *Tikkun olam* tells us the same thing. We are supposed to make the world a better place in even one small way through our actions.

For you, this is a wonderful opportunity! And not in the same way that teachers start the year off and say enthusiastically, "Oh, you're going to have

**"For my bat mitzvah project I volunteered
at the Oakmont Wild Animal Preserve."**

such a wonderful time in class this year learning the quadratic formula!"
In that case, you're stuck working on something that's already decided by
someone else. If you happen to love math, then you really might have a
great time. But the poor kids who just don't do as well in math, and prefer
to spend all of their time reading and writing stories are probably not in for
as much fun.

Finding a connection to some kind of community service project,
though, is all about *you* and what you like. Some students love animals, so
they volunteer their time in an animal shelter (and some go on to become
veterinarians). Others are crazy about working with little kids, so they find
a way to help out in day care centers or other after-school settings (and
later consider teaching careers). The more business-minded kids find a way
to raise funds for worthwhile causes (and are destined to become temple
presidents).

For other kids, it may be more of a mixture of activities. You could
spend a few hours helping out in your Hebrew school or local Jewish Federation offices. In addition, you might collect school supplies for needy kids

INSIDER'S TIP!

WHAT IF your temple doesn't have any requirement like this?

You might consider taking on some kind of *tzedakah* project anyway. Remember that the beauty of this suggestion isn't to make some adult happy or blindly fulfill another in a long list of requirements. You have the opportunity to do something positive and constructive in an area that means something to *you*. Even suggesting to your parents that you donate a portion of your bar mitzvah money toward a worthwhile fund of your choice can be a significant statement of who you are and what's important in your life.

or join with some other volunteers to clean up a neglected section of your neighborhood. This is a way for you to mold some positive activity around your own personality.

I have had some students who, years after the bar mitzvah, remember next to nothing about how to lead a service but recall very fondly that they played basketball with underprivileged children as part of their *tzedakah* project. That may have been the one connection they made. It not only made a lasting impression but also planted the seed for future charitable acts.

Assuming that your temple has some sort of obligation like this for you to perform, don't just groan and look at it like it's just one more meaningless piece of homework that some adult thinks you need to do. Instead, think about what you love to do. (If you told me that you love to spend all afternoon texting with your friends, I'd suggest that you find a way to collect used cell phones for those who can't afford them. See?) The goal here is to connect *yourself* to having a bar mitzvah.

The Prayers

The prayer book is filled with beautiful poetry, plaintive pleas, and eloquent words of praise. You don't have to be a liturgical scholar to understand much of what's written there. Nor do you have to believe in the specific words to really appreciate the emotions and images that might come to mind. You might find a certain text, even *one line*, to be so meaningful that it stays with you long after the bar mitzvah is over, the checks are cashed, and you've outgrown your suit.

Many years ago, I was teaching my Hebrew school class about *Birchot Hashachar*, the blessings of the morning (discussed in detail in chapter 5). One line caught the attention of a particular student that afternoon.

Blessed are you, God, who opens the eyes of the blind.

The context of this blessing is that we are reciting words of praise for all the things that we might otherwise take for granted first thing in the morning. Among these are waking up and realizing that it's morning, opening your eyes, and getting out of bed. So this blessing presumably thanks God that each morning we can open our eyes after sleeping and see things around us once again.

That sounds pretty straightforward.

But this student initiated a discussion that completely pre-empted anything else I had planned to talk about that day by asking a simple question:

What if you're blind and can't see?

What an amazing question that was.

Does a blind person recite words that praise God for giving sight to the blind? Do we, in good conscience, say these words knowing that many people are born blind, or become blind because of accident or sickness, and will never see again? Might a blind person be exempt from this prayer? Is it cruel for us to take pleasure in our ability to see when we might be sitting in temple next to someone who can't?

Well, we went on and on about possible interpretations of this prayer. Perhaps giving sight to the blind refers to the invention of Braille, which lets a blind person "see." Or the expertise of medical professionals and inventors of technology that might treat diseases of the eyes either now or in the future. Maybe blindness wasn't meant to be taken literally but rather was a metaphor for ignorance, which could be cured not with light but with enlightenment. These are wonderful thoughts, and they help to demonstrate the myriad ways of understanding any text.

This one line resonated strongly in the head and heart of that student. This was the one connection that she took with her throughout her bat mitzvah training and service. That's not to say that she cared about and remembered nothing else. But in the future, whenever she opens a prayer book and sees this particular blessing, she will connect right back to her bat mitzvah time.

There are so many other opportunities to find a connection that might not even involve the meaning of the words. Sometimes the choreography of the service, ways that we move or make certain actions, can provide great significance (see chapter 5). When you recite the words of the *Shema*, it is traditional to close or cover your eyes in order to better concentrate on the meaning of the words. Some students love that! I have found that even some of the more jaded and distracted (OK, misbehaving) kids really feel something when they close their eyes and are alone, even if it's only for ten seconds. They've connected with the *Shema*.

During another part of the service, it's customary to raise yourself on tiptoes three times in a row, each of the three times you recite the word *kadosh* ("holy"). A lot of kids have seen this done in services many times, thought it looked kind of funny, but never knew *why* people were doing it. After learning that we raise ourselves up to try to make ourselves just a little bit holier, like the angels on high that we're reading about just then, the action goes from being a source of amusement to something meaningful that kids can understand.

I remember a talk given by a teacher of mine a looong time ago when I was studying to become a cantor. Well, "remember" might be overstating it a bit. At this point, I don't particularly recall most of what he talked about. Except for one thing. He made a point that we, as cantors, had a unique opportunity to add holiness to the services and to the Jewish community. In one prayer, we read that the angels on high also try to add holiness, described while reciting the words, *Kadosh Kadosh Kadosh*. And as my teacher said these words, he raised himself up on his toes as if he was actually reciting the prayer. It was such an apt comparison, and so beautifully presented, that it has remained with me ever since. Additionally, I often think of him and that talk whenever I'm leading the service and get to that page and recite those words. Such is the power of one connection.

Here's a Portion for You

We haven't even gotten to the Torah or haftarah yet. From the beginning of your lessons, you are instantly connected with your particular Torah portion (even if it's the leprosy one). Adults will always ask you, "What *parsha* do you have?" Then they'll tell you what their *parsha* was (and that the haftarah went on for twenty-three pages and they had to sing it with no vowels, in the dark, during a blizzard, and while being chased by drunken Cossacks).

As you learn about your Torah portion, you may be moved to further understand more about some of the characters, the location, or even some ancient history. (Or you may enjoy reading about leprosy so much that you decide to become a dermatologist.) Perhaps you share a name with one of the characters (Jacob, Joseph, Deborah, Rachel, Jezebel . . .) and want to know more about what that person did and whether you share any personality traits as well.

The story of Joseph and his brothers is particularly well known. It's the ultimate story of how a parent (Jacob) completely messed up his family by favoring one child above all the others. When I ask my students if they ever feel that Mom and Dad treat a brother or sister better than them, I immediately get a very enthusiastic response, and then I know that this story has made an impression.

The Music

Considering the fact that you spend a great percentage of your time learning how to chant every prayer and sing all the tropes, I think it's amazing that we haven't even gotten around to discussing anything musical yet. Obviously, different tunes and melodies make up a huge part of your bar mitzvah training and service, and there are numerous opportunities for you to find a way to connect.

There may be a specific congregational melody that you love. Even if you don't know much about the prayer or remember when it's recited, you know that you love the tune and like to sing it. Often a prayer is so well known that there are a lot of different tunes that people know for singing it. One example is the closing hymn of the service, *Adon Olam*. Because the text is written in a simple and metrical way, it lends itself easily to almost any tune you want to put with it. Students will occasionally figure out that they can sing *Adon Olam* to the latest pop song or a favorite TV theme song. Some cantors will let them sing it that way in services (although I'm not one of them . . . sorry). Still, I love the fact that a student will connect enough with the rhythm of the words and suggest a new way to sing them.

I have had families make special requests for specific tunes to other prayers, either because they're the tunes they remember from their own childhood, or they just know and love that melody. Whenever I can, I accommodate those requests. I have, on occasion, had to learn completely new tunes just so I could sing what someone wanted. That's a win-win for everyone, isn't it?

Music has a particularly powerful ability to create connections, and some endure forever. Many years ago, I used to present a weekly program in a Jewish nursing home. Each Friday afternoon, I would walk into different

JUST FOR PARENTS

ON THE OTHER end of the spectrum are cantors who refuse to make any changes or any accommodations for parents' requests. Let's separate some simple requests from what might be considered micromanaging.

If you have a favorite melody that you remember, and wonder whether it's something that your child could sing in services instead of your temple's "traditional" tune, that's a perfectly reasonable request. Your cantor might have legitimate reasons to politely say no (for instance, maybe the tune isn't appropriate for the text), but there is no harm in asking.

Unfortunately, some cantors feel that agreeing to even the most harmless favor will eventually mean that they won't be able to say no to anyone. They might feel that they need to demonstrate the fact that they're in charge by never taking input about the musical content of services from anyone. As you might imagine, I don't feel that this attitude is in the least part constructive or educational for anyone. Rather than encouraging parents and students to make connections, this approach puts obstacles in the way.

Then again, don't make a request to skip a prayer because you don't like it or tell the cantor that you don't want him to sing a certain tune. I once had a parent tell me to sing along with the congregational tunes more softly so that people could hear her son better.

Um . . . micromanaging.

units and create a Shabbat experience, which included lighting candles, making the *Kiddush* and *motzi* (the blessings over wine and challah), and singing some traditional Friday night melodies. The residents loved to participate and I think it was something they looked forward to each week.

One unit that I visited each week housed residents suffering from Alzheimer's disease or other forms of dementia. Obviously, they weren't able to participate the same way as others could, and of course many weren't even aware of what I was doing there or what any of my actions meant.

Still, one thing sticks with me to this day. When I would start singing some very traditional melodies, some otherwise unresponsive patients would begin to focus on me, become more alert, and start to mouth or even sing along with the words! The nurses and other professionals who worked the unit confirmed for me that this might be the *only time all week* that they observed any response from some of these unfortunate residents.

Talk about making connections.

Come to Your Five Senses

If all of Jewish prayer and learning consisted of standing or sitting still and listening to some person run through the *Siddur*, it would never have lasted through the years. Luckily, much of what we do in temple involves not just listening but the other senses as well. These can provide powerful connections.

One of the disadvantages of going to temple regularly (I bet you didn't think I'd point out any of those!) is that over time, you lose a sense of wonder and newness associated with the experience. Some Jews have rarely seen the inside of a Torah scroll, and when they do, they're amazed at the look of the parchment and the ornate calligraphy of the text. If they are given the chance to hold the scroll in their arms, they do so with trepidation and even awe. Although I love being as familiar and knowledgable about the Jewish tradition as I am, sometimes I wish I could get even a fraction of that feeling back.

That sense of awe can and does happen, and I find that these instances are connected with various senses. Because the Torah scroll is written on parchment, some scrolls might have a slightly musty smell. Nothing unpleasant—almost like an old book that you find on the shelf that hasn't been opened in years. Every now and then, I'll open up the Torah and that particular Toromah (yes, I totally made that word up: Torah + aroma = Toromah) will waft up and I'll instantly be transported back to my childhood temple and remember what it was like to be a kid and look into a Torah scroll.

It's more than just nostalgia, which is a nice feeling but by definition is something that is concerned with the past. Instead, the connection that I feel lets me appreciate the Torah more, as it links me with the past. It becomes something intergenerational, able to endure over the years. I can get all that from just a quick smell of parchment.

The sense of touch is also something that we can use a lot during services. One of my favorite rituals is putting on *tefillin*. For those who have never seen this done, it looks pretty unusual. *Tefillin* are small black boxes, with black leather straps, which are wrapped a certain way around one's arm and then placed upon the head. This is done to fulfill the directions in the Torah to "bind the commandments upon your arm and between your eyes." The *tefillin* are worn at each morning service, except for Shabbat and other holidays. Because they are not used on Shabbat, many Jews are completely unfamiliar with this ritual.

I happen to find this practice very meaningful, in that it adds something tactile, using our sense of touch, to an otherwise bland service. (The weekday morning service is usually pretty plain and done quickly. Nothing fancy. Everyone has to get to work or school.) Wearing *tefillin*, however, adds a special element to the experience, by letting the worshipper use another part of his body to connect to services.

There are also many times in the service that revolve around the senses of taste and smell. The *havdalah* service on Saturday evening, which marks the end of Shabbat and the beginning of the rest of the week, utilizes a spice box, which gets passed around so that everyone has a chance to smell the spices. Anyone who's ever attended services for the Jewish holiday of *Sukkot* knows that the etrog (a kind of citrus fruit that looks very much like a lemon) that we use has a powerful and wonderful smell. Even just the act of making *Kiddush* and sipping that really sweet kosher wine can provide a strong connection.

The Bottom Line

Remember what I told you in chapter 10. You have two choices how you make your way through the bar mitzvah. The first is the passive way, just letting everything happen to you and hoping for the best. You're relieved when it's over, and you might realize that you did a great job, but that's the end of it. You haven't really changed at all.

The other alternative is to take the active approach. *Find* something to connect with. *Change* how you look at things. *Decide* what's important to you. Remember that this isn't just a huge test that you have to pass, after which you can relax and go back to your regular life. Being responsible for some important decisions *is* your regular life from now on.

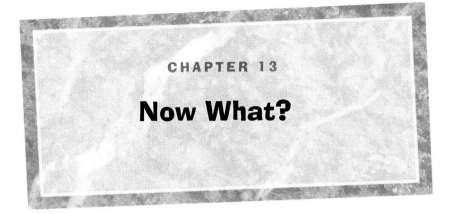

Now What?

WARNING: *You're about to read a joke that's so old, I think Moses told it to the Israelites.*

There was a synagogue that had a mice problem. They tried everything to get rid of these pesky mice. They used traps. They used chemicals. They called exterminators. Nothing worked. Finally, in exasperation, the congregants turned to the rabbi and asked for any advice he could give. He said, "I'll take care of the shul's mice problem." He arranged for all of the mice to have a bar mitzvah. After it was over, he said, "The problem's solved. You'll never see the mice again."

Of course, old or not, the best Jewish jokes are the ones that have an element of truth in them, and this one, unfortunately, is right up there. It is a sad but common fact of Jewish life that kids and families have a tendency to disappear from the synagogue after the bar mitzvah is over. There are a variety of reasons why this is the case. Let's take a look at some of them, as well as figure out some ways that you can still remain involved.

This does beg the question: Why remain involved? In fact, it's such a good question that I think I'll devote the next section just to that.

Why Remain Involved?

If the bar mitzvah service is over, then you can safely assume that you have completed a huge list of accomplishments. First, you may have been attending your temple's religious school one, two, or even three days a week since an early grade. On top of that, you had lessons every week for several months before your big day. You and your family attended services, if not on a regular basis, then at least a lot more often than usual. You performed some act of community service or completed a project.

How about all the material you learned? You had to master numerous prayers and parts of the service, both the words and the melodies, as well as all of the trope symbols. You then stood in front of an entire room full of people, most of whom were there for no other reason than to stare at you and listen to you sing.

And we haven't even gotten to your parents yet. They've probably been planning this bar mitzvah for a lot longer than your lessons lasted. They had to find and then book a party location, caterer, DJ . . . It's safe to say that everyone in the house had their hands full. Even little brothers and sisters who seemed to have no worries in the world finally figured out that in a few years they would have to go through this whole thing themselves.

I'm tired just from writing all that. I can imagine how the average family must feel after a bar or bat mitzvah.

Maybe instead of asking why remain involved, I should consider it a miracle if anyone actually does come back to shul after the bar mitzvah is over.

Clearly, it's easy to experience burnout. For months, you and your family have lived, breathed, slept, bickered, eaten, and probably dreamed *bar mitzvah*. It's not unreasonable to say, "Thank goodness that's over! We need a break from all that."

The flaw in that logic, though, is that you're looking at your bar mitzvah as the end point. You got there. You did it. Great. Now you're done.

But you know that's not really the case, don't you? Even a young kid knows that a bar mitzvah means that you are now a Jewish adult. We've already talked all about that. You may not be able to drive, vote, or order a drink, but you have other obligations. You have to start observing some rituals and traditions and, even more importantly, make educated decisions about how you want to live your Jewish life. Even assuming those decisions will change a lot as time goes on, this is when that process begins.

So if the day after the bar mitzvah is really the *last* time you think you'll end up doing anything Jewish, then that really doesn't make much sense, does it?

We're back to looking at your bar mitzvah as a huge test. You studied. You prepared. You did it. You passed. Done.

Notice that I keep asking about remaining involved. I could have phrased the question, "Why keep coming to services?" I know you think that all cantors and rabbis care about is whether you come to services. But I want to emphasize the fact that the most important post–bar mitzvah decision you can make is to stay connected. That certainly may mean attending services. It could also mean a host of other activities that have nothing to do with attending services, like volunteering, joining a Jewish youth group, or finding more opportunities for Jewish learning, as well as many more possibilities.

The Thirteen-Year-Old Jew

If you don't make an effort to remain involved, then you have effectively frozen yourself at age thirteen forever. Now, it's true that adults are always interested in looking younger, but if you ask anyone what age they would like to remain forever, thirteen would *not* be a top answer. Yet, most temples have congregations filled with thirteen-year-old Jews of all ages. These thirteen-year-olds sit on the boards, make decisions, and hire the rabbi and cantor. Oh sure, they may look like adults, but inside, they're only carrying around the Jewish education and knowledge of their first thirteen years.

Can you imagine if we allowed that in other important settings?

The nuclear power plant in your area would be run by people who never got past learning about electrons. The symphony orchestra that presents concerts would keep on playing Beethoven's Fifth Symphony because it's the only piece they learned. Libraries and bookstores would be filled only with books about vampires and wizards. Oh wait, that last one is actually true now.

You get the idea. Why would you take something as important as Judaism and consider it so insignificant that you're done learning anything more after you're thirteen years old?

Let's take an example. One of those durable images and traditions in Jewish life is the so-called Book of Life. Every Rosh Hashanah, Jews are supposed to engage in the act of repentance, which is a fancy way of saying that you should think about all the things you did wrong over the past year, apologize, and decide that you're going to do better in the future. We also learn that it is at this important time of year that God compiles a pretty important list. God decides which names end up in the Book of Life and which ones don't. Perhaps it has to do with every person's actions over the past year, or maybe it's more random. But one part of the text does lead us to believe that we can try to shift things our way by performing repentance.

This is a great way to understand God and the idea of reward and punishment—if you're about seven years old. It's what I call the Santa Claus model of God. You picture some old guy, probably with a flowing white beard, who is watching everyone to see if they've been naughty or nice. If you've been good, then you get rewarded (Book of Life), but if you've been bad, then you get punished (Game Over).

There's a reason Santa Claus is such a popular legend for little kids. Your average child isn't very good at higher thinking or abstractions. We do the same thing with Jewish themes—we simplify them so they become

JUST FOR PARENTS

Now I'M treading on dangerous waters, because I'm calling an entire belief system into question. There are, in fact, many functional, intelligent, and highly educated Jewish adults who do have this notion of reward and punishment.

To me, these beliefs can take on absurd extremes. There are some Jews who maintain that if a house burned down, it was the result of the *mezuzot* on the doorposts not being mounted or maintained properly. More recently, when the space shuttle *Columbia*, carrying Israeli astronaut Ilan Ramon, burned up upon re-entry, killing all aboard, there were some Jews who suggested that perhaps there was a connection between that terrible event and the fact that the shuttle was flying on Shabbat, which would be a violation of traditional Jewish law.

I simply can't subscribe to this thinking. I feel that the challenge of any Jewish person, regardless of denomination and level of observance, is to constantly interpret, change, and mold our sacred texts and prayers to try to find meaning. No matter how one chooses to believe in God (if at all), I can't connect to the notion of a vengeful God who looks for any opportunity to cause pain and suffering.

accessible to young children. I don't think a Hebrew school teacher would do very well in her first grade class if she tried to lead a discussion on why righteous people occasionally suffer or die.

Because it's become common for kids to halt their Jewish education at age thirteen, after they become bar mitzvah, there are a ton of people who may be professional, educated, and highly informed but are walking around with the Jewish education of a seventh grader.

Do you want to spend your entire Jewish life as a seventh grader?

There's a whole world of knowledge out there for you. I told you back in chapter 11 that you might think of Judaism as a giant banquet table full of varied and unfamiliar dishes. You have the ability to decide what you want to have and what you would prefer to leave. When you walk out of the temple after your bar mitzvah and rarely, if ever, come back, you deny yourself that chance to taste new dishes. It's like you've decided to eat nothing but peanut butter and jelly for the rest of your life.

What You Can Do

First, it's OK to do nothing. You've just run the Jewish version of a marathon, and every marathon runner knows that you have to give yourself time to rest and recover after completing such an achievement. Take a break. Enjoy having a few more free hours a week. Take some time to argue with your parents that you should be able to use at least some of your bar or bat mitzvah money to buy yourself something cool (computer, iPad, cell phone, jewelry, new car that you can drive in four years), rather than "wasting" all that money in some boring college fund where all it does is sit there and earn interest.

Then, your first opportunity to remain involved will come up naturally without your having to do much. You probably will be attending other b'nei mitzvah services either for other kids in your Hebrew school class or for some of your Jewish classmates at school. Of course, this will vary depending on when your bar mitzvah was and how many Jewish kids you know. If you assume that most b'nei mitzvah take place over the course of the school year, then a kid with a September or October date will be able to be a relaxed guest at all the other ones that follow, whereas a May or June kid will have to sit through an entire year's worth of services worrying about their turn. So it does vary.

I would urge you not to waste this opportunity. Assuming that you've successfully finished your bar mitzvah and are now a happy, worry-free guest at a friend's, there are some easy ways for you to remain involved. Instead of spending the whole two or three hours talking to your friends (and getting *shushed* by all the adults) and texting everyone (and getting nasty looks from the other congregants), why not try something really crazy? Why not listen and pay attention to the service?

Now, I'm not really living on the planet Mars. I understand that there you are, sitting with all of your friends, many of whom aren't Jewish and would have no clue as to what's going on even if they were paying attention. I don't realistically expect that while everyone else is whispering and keeping themselves occupied you're going to sit there, singing loudly and praying fervently along with the congregation the whole time. Still, it's possible to tune in to what's going on in the service.

Have a little fun. Play "detective" while you're sitting in the congregation. Picture your favorite crime drama on TV. At the crime scene, the lead detectives show up, pull out their little spiral notebooks, and start asking questions. Pretend that you're the lead detective and you're trying to find clues about this service and how it might be different from when you did your service. That actually might take a little bit of detective work on your part. After all, your bar mitzvah and this one where you're sitting in the congregation are probably both taking place on a Shabbat morning. Therefore, the prayers would be the same. What you had to sing and what this kid has to sing is likely identical. At first glance, it's the very same service—just replace the bar mitzvah kid and of course all the relatives and guests.

It becomes even more interesting when you get the chance to attend friends' b'nei mitzvah at various synagogues. Every temple is a little different, and that becomes even more obvious when you're comparing Reform and Conservative synagogues. For instance, if you're not used to using any musical instruments as part of the Shabbat service, it can be pretty surprising to hear a cantor sing with a guitar.

Now dig a little deeper. Is the Torah reading the same? How about the haftarah? (Hint: No, they won't be the same.) What is this new Torah reading about? Did you hear any new melodies this week that you don't recognize? Was it *Rosh Chodesh*? Did they take out just one Torah scroll from the ark, or more than one?

Then check out the crowd. Do a lot of them seem familiar with the service? Are a lot of people singing? Are most people looking around, unsure of what's going on? Is anything else taking place in temple other than your friend's bar mitzvah? Is anyone being honored or called to the Torah for a special occasion?

If you try to answer these and other questions that you might come up with, all of a sudden you're completely tuned into the service. You're going to start picking up more details, a lot of which you probably missed because you were so nervous and distracted during your bar mitzvah. This is a great way to continue learning about the service.

Don't stop there. Take a few glances into the *Siddur* that you're holding. Even if you have trouble following the whole service, pages are usually announced often enough that you can figure out where you are. See if you recognize what's being chanted. Was it something you did during your bar mitzvah? Do you remember it? This time you have the luxury of being able to look over at the English translation, so why not check out what that paragraph says. Unfortunately, sometimes the English is hard to decipher as well. Can you figure out a way to put it in your own words?

Look! You're already continuing your Jewish education and all you had to do was pay attention to the service. It's that easy.

The Incredible Shrinking Class

There's nothing more depressing than being a seventh-grade Hebrew school teacher.

This poor teacher prepares great lessons, loves to teach Jewish kids, and gets to watch his class get smaller and smaller as the year goes on. Over the course of the year, fewer and fewer kids come to class. The lessons remain interesting and educational; there are just not as many students to benefit from them.

Why is this? Is this some strange temple flu that only infects seventh-graders and claims them one by one? Should we wear masks?

You know the real answer. Some kids stop coming to Hebrew school after they've had their bar mitzvah. Maybe the kid convinced their parents ("But *no one* comes afterward!") or the parents themselves stop making the effort to drive them. Perhaps when lessons ended, all of their other regular activities—soccer, music, dance, gymnastics—rushed in to fill the gap, and just like that, they're busier than ever.

If you stop coming to Hebrew school, then what you're saying is that you've already learned everything you need to. Everything that takes place now in class doesn't matter, since it won't benefit how you do at your bar mitzvah. You've now committed yourself to be a thirteen-year-old Jew for the foreseeable future.

Instead, try this: If your bar mitzvah takes place early in the school year, make sure that you still attend your Hebrew school sessions until the end of the school year. (And by the way, this also sets a great example for your friends and classmates who, after seeing you there, will be less apt themselves to stop attending.) During your Hebrew school classes, try to find some connection between what's being discussed and anything that you learned during lessons or about services. Remember, it's all about finding connections.

And what about when seventh grade is over? Many synagogues have religious school programs for older kids, often right through high school. Because the students are older and more mature, you will likely have the opportunity to learn some really interesting subjects, presented in ways you've never seen before. Depending on your temple's educational program, you might have the opportunity to take courses where you learn about Jewish sports heroes or actors, cooking, music, ethics, or many other really interesting subjects which are intended for older and more mature students.

Keep on Coming!

Right now, many of my suggestions involve coming to services. Why not? You're now something of an expert on what goes on in temple. In many cases, you may know a lot more than anyone else in your family. You've got a lot of momentum going, so why let all that go to waste?

There are a lot of easy, painless ways to continue your participation in services. First, the most obvious suggestion is to simply attend. If Saturday morning isn't convenient for your family, then come Friday night. Your temple may have short morning or evening services during the week or on Sunday. Usually these last a fraction of the time of a Shabbat service (I can get through a weekday evening service in ten minutes). In the process, you'll become familiar with another type of service in a low-stress, informal environment.

This is probably one of the best ways you can choose to remain involved, because it benefits everyone. Obviously, you will continue to learn about the service and the prayers just by sitting there, and it doesn't require much effort on your part at all. But more importantly, you're also demonstrating that you're taking your new responsibilities seriously.

One of the most significant differences between your pre–bar mitzvah self and your new Jewish adult self is the fact that you are now counted in a *minyan*. All services need at least ten people so that all of the prayers, especially the Mourners' Kaddish, may be recited. Often, synagogues have these daily or evening services so that congregants who need to say the Kaddish have a place to do so. And there needs to be a *minyan* present.

Where do you think these ten people come from? They're regular temple people who like to come or know that others are depending on them to help out. They make an effort to attend at least some of the time. Now that you're over the age of thirteen, that becomes something that you should think about as well.

Other Kinds of Services

While we're already feeling so cheerful talking about the Mourners' Kaddish, let me point out another opportunity for you to make an enormous difference in the lives of other members of your congregation, just by showing up somewhere.

After a person dies, it's customary for the family to sit shiva at their home for a certain period of time. Often it's seven days, but could be a shorter time. During that period, the family has to recite the Mourners' Kaddish, but because of the rules of shiva, they aren't really supposed to leave the house to come to temple. So we bring the temple to them!

The rabbi, cantor, and other congregants will come to the house each day or evening, bringing a set of prayer books for everyone to use, and they'll lead a little service right there in the living room.

Where do you come in?

Hopefully through the front door. There may be times when your parents have to pay a shiva call to the home of a friend or relative, and now, if

INSIDER'S TIP!

ALL THIS talk about Mourners' Kaddish and people dying is pretty depressing. While I'm using these examples right now simply to highlight the importance of having a *minyan* present during certain occasions, many Jews really base their participation in synagogue around mourning. I think that's too bad.

Take some average family. The kids are older, so they are out of the bar mitzvah world. They come to temple on the High Holidays along with everyone else, but we don't really see them very often otherwise. Then, unfortunately, they have a death in the family. Even after the funeral and shiva, there are other times during the year when they have to mark the occasion of this person's death.

First, they are supposed to recite Kaddish for a certain period of time, and then again every year on the anniversary of the death. This is referred to by the Yiddish word *yahrzeit*. Additionally, there are four times a year when a memorial prayer called *Yizkor* is recited in services. Many congregants make a special effort to attend these services in order to say *Yizkor*.

So what's the problem?

At first, nothing at all. The beauty of the Jewish tradition is that it requires an aspect of mourning to be done in temple, with a *minyan*, and not done privately. Otherwise, people who were very sad might never make the effort to leave the house. So the laws were set up intelligently and with a keen eye on human nature.

I have found, though, that sometimes congregants come to services only for reasons of mourning. The *yahrzeit* date. Time to say Kaddish. Have to recite *Yizkor*. Over time, they associate services and praying with sadness.

you attend with them, you can be counted in the *minyan* that is required to say the Mourners' Kaddish. It's another way you can attend services without even going to temple.

You Could Even Participate

Let's take this one step further. In addition to coming to services on some kind of regular basis (which would be great), you could even participate in the services. After all, haven't you just spent months learning and memorizing a ton of prayers and melodies? If you just forget them, that's kind of a waste, isn't it?

There are probably numerous opportunities for you to actually *do* something in services. Don't worry, we won't make you put on makeup and do your hair and wear horribly uncomfortable clothes and all that other stuff. But many temples try to keep the post–b'nei mitzvah kids involved by having them read Torah again—and soon, before they forget how.

The beauty of Torah reading is that the portions that you're assigned are often nice and short, sometimes as little as three sentences. It's a great way to keep your skills sharp and remain involved in services (while looking really good in front of the congregation) without too much effort.

Your synagogue may have an organized way to keep track of all the teenagers that come back and read Torah on a regular basis. Maybe after you read a certain number of times, or a specific number of sentences, you will be recognized with your name in print in the temple bulletin or newsletter, or even a small presentation, like a book or gift card.

Once you become experienced at Torah reading (which will happen very quickly), it's a skill that you'll use constantly. I have had a good number of former students return to tell me that when they attended services at college (even if their parents "encouraged" them to do so), they were soon asked to either lead the service or read the Torah when everyone else figured out that they could do those things. "Cantor, I was the only one there who knew how to read Torah!"

Best words ever.

More Community Service

Of course, it's not all about coming to services. Since you probably performed some community service project or something similar while you were busy preparing for your bar mitzvah, you have a perfect opportunity to continue along those lines.

One of the main points of encouraging or requiring you to do this project was to show you that being a responsible and adult member of the Jewish community involves a *lot* more than showing up to services (even though that's pretty important too).

INSIDER'S TIP!

DON'T FORGET that *all* of these ideas on how to remain involved can be done with your friends.

Sure, I know that you're not likely to become the most popular kid in your class when you text your friends Friday afternoon, "hey lets all go 2 shul 2nite 4 services." But there's nothing wrong with making service attendance or community involvement something that you plan with your friends. There are certainly families that call each other and find out who's doing what, or which kids might be coming to certain services. I happen to love it when some families attend on a Friday night, for instance, and the kids immediately leave their parents and sit together. That makes it a much more social and enjoyable experience for everyone.

I have had students connect so well to their projects that they stayed involved for years afterward. Some kids became such effective fundraisers that they put those skills to work raising more money for other worthy causes within (or even outside of) the Jewish community.

Does your synagogue have any kind of social action or community service committee? It can often be a lot easier for a big group of people to organize a project than for one person. Can you imagine how happy the members of this committee would be to see a recent bar mitzvah kid walk into a meeting?

Youth Groups

One of the most rewarding and enjoyable ways that you can maintain a connection to Jewish life is to join a youth group, such as USY (United Synagogue Youth), BBYO (B'nai B'rith Youth Organization), or NFTY (North American Federation of Temple Youth). It might depend on your specific temple as to which group(s) you have access to.

These groups are wonderful ways to connect with other Jewish kids in your community, many of which you may already know from school. You might attend parties, go on fun outings, or perform some acts of community service. You'll be able to attend conventions or overnights, all within the context of Jewish life. These groups have been around a long time for the very simple reason that they're fun for teenagers.

Over the years, I have seen numerous lifelong friendships formed from these youth groups.

The Bottom Line

Whether it's attending services, continuing your Jewish education, joining your temple's youth group, or getting involved with a worthy social action cause, it's vitally important that you not let the day of your bar mitzvah mark the last time you set foot in temple or remain an active member of the Jewish community.

If you've read this whole book, it was because you knew that having a bar mitzvah and getting through it (in one piece) were really important. I think it's pretty normal for most of your attention to be concentrated on preparing for and successfully navigating those critical two or three hours when you're the sole focus of attention. Hopefully, along the way, while you got through this book and during your study and preparation, you also learned that there's a lot more that should come after as well.

I started the very first chapter of this book by explaining what the term bar or bat mitzvah means and how you should think about it. Whether it's a throwback to an earlier era, or a giant cosmic joke suggested by a mischievous angel, age thirteen is actually a pretty sensible time to begin taking Judaism and its responsibilities more seriously.

This is when you start thinking about what kind of person you're going to be. You probably don't do this intentionally—"I have decided to become a caring and sensitive human being!"—but rather gradually, as you decide what kind of friends you have, how you talk to your parents, what subjects you love in school, and how seriously you take your homework. All of these aspects of your personality are things that your parents would love to decide for you but can't. Similarly, even though your parents might be able to require you to come to temple at certain times, eventually these decisions will be yours to make.

Having your bar mitzvah was just the first step.

APPENDIX I

The Ultimate Insider's Quick Hints and Tricks

YEAH, I know you. This is what you really wanted to find out. Not all that stuff about responsibility and trope and the Jewish calendar. Well, that's why I put this material in the back of the book tucked away in the Appendix. If I had made this the first chapter, would you have kept reading?

Here, then, are some tried and true hints, tricks, and strategies to make your few hours in front of everyone go as smoothly as possible. In many cases, they're as simple and straightforward as can be, but if you keep them in mind, you'll have a much easier time.

Insider's Quick Hint #1: Sing along with the congregation

There are lots of times during the service when the congregation is supposed to sing along. This can take one of two forms. Either everyone is singing a congregational melody together or else you're leading a responsive prayer, in which you chant one part, the congregation sings the next, and you go back and forth. One example of that is the *Ashrei*, which is often sung line by line, with you and the congregation taking turns.

It's tempting to just take a break when everyone else is singing. But you should sing along with the congregation, even if it's quietly or under your breath. If you don't, it's easy to get distracted and lose your place in the prayer book. Then all of a sudden it's your turn to sing and you have no idea where you are, and you either freeze or come in at the wrong place. If you're singing along with everyone, even if it's just in your head, you will never lose your place.

Insider's Quick Hint #2: Don't worry about the past

This is something that I learned while I was studying for my pilot's license. As the aviator's saying goes, "The two most useless things in the world are the runway behind you and the fuel you left back in the pumps." In other words, there comes a point when worrying about something in the past ("Gee, now that I'm trying to take off, I sure wish I had a longer runway. Oops!") is just fruitless. So don't bother.

In fact, it becomes downright distracting. When you're on page 132, it doesn't do you any good to figure out whether you botched page 90 or sang it correctly. It will, however, take your attention away from what you're doing now.

If it's in the past, just forget about it. If you got it right, great. If you did make a mistake, it's not a big deal.

Insider's Quick Hint #3: But do worry about the future

Make sure that you're never surprised when you turn the page.

I once noticed a bat mitzvah girl do an amazing thing. As she was singing or reading a page in the *Siddur,* she would occasionally sneak a peek at the next page. She wanted to know what was coming up. I thought that was brilliant! I never told her to do that; she simply figured out that it was helpful to know what was coming up.

Your brain can only work so fast, especially when you're already dealing with the mental stress of having to remember so much material. I will often watch a bar mitzvah kid get a momentary "deer-in-the-headlights" look when they turn the page and have to figure out what prayer they're looking at, how to sing it, and where to come in. Just by taking a quick look at the next page you can prevent that from happening.

Insider's Quick Hint #4: And get that page turn ready

While we're talking about pages, this just in from the Department of the Obvious: When you get to the last word on a page, you need to turn the page.

Why, oh why, then, do I see student after student chant a page, get to the bottom, and just wait?

"Oh, did you want me to go on?"

"Noooo, we'll just stare at this page for the next hour or so."

Or at her bat mitzvah, a student will be singing through a prayer that starts on one page and continues to the next, so she does know that she is supposed to actually turn the page. But then she gets to the last word on the first page and starts fumbling and rustling and trying to turn that stubborn page so she can go on. Meanwhile, a good ten or fifteen seconds have gone by, and the prayer has been interrupted.

No matter what is on the next page, whether it's a continuation of your part or something that another person leads—get the page turn ready. While you are in the middle of whatever you're singing, just get a finger under the next page. It's something you can absentmindedly do while you're busy concentrating on your present task, and it will make everything run much more smoothly.

Insider's Quick Hint #5: Put your hands on the table

Ugh, who likes to be reminded about posture? Stand up straight! Don't slouch! Stop shuffling your feet!

It's hard to stand up at the podium on the *bimah* for however many hours and maintain decent posture. But if you don't, it just doesn't look good. You've spent so much time and effort preparing and studying, and you're going to waste a lot of it, slouched over the table with your head down mumbling into the book. Your parents will be upset with you, and then they'll be upset with me for not getting you to stand up straighter, as if I have some magic power over your posture.

Do this instead: When you stand at the podium, simply take both of your hands and put them palm down on the table, one in front of each leg. That instantly makes you stand up straight with no effort, plus it has the added benefit of giving you a place for your hands, so you don't start putting them in your pockets or holding them in front of you like you have to go to the bathroom. Which brings us to . . .

Insider's Quick Hint #6: Go to the bathroom

Before services. Even if you don't have to. 'Nuff said.

Insider's Quick Hint #7: Slow down if you need to

This is not me telling you to slow down because you're speeding through the service. I've already mentioned that even if I could remind you repeatedly to slow down, you're likely to simply resume whatever pace is natural and comfortable.

Some kids, when they sing for long periods of time, start to get out of breath. This is particularly a concern when you're chanting your haftarah, which is one long, extended solo, with no breaks. Once you begin to get out of breath, it starts to become a distraction, plus it affects your singing.

If this happens, the trick is to immediately slow down. Just start taking your time with each word. You don't have to worry about maintaining this much slower pace for long. Just tell yourself that you're going to take your time for a little while. After all, no one's going anywhere until you're done, right?

This strategy will get your breathing right back on track.

Insider's Quick Hint #8: Don't add words

How about this bar mitzvah speech: "I would like to thunk—oops! I mean thank my parents and my little sis—no, I mean brother for . . ."

If you catch yourself in a mistake while you're singing or reciting something, all you need to do is simply correct it. That's it. You don't need any comment or apology. This might be the hardest hint of all because a lot of the time, you just don't have control over it. It's a nervous habit. Nevertheless, just try to be aware.

The very best way to incorporate this hint is during your lessons when you're running through material that you know pretty well, but you still might make an occasional mistake. See if you can get yourself in the habit of either ignoring the mistake (your teacher will stop and correct you if he needs to) or making a quick and seamless correction.

Insider's Quick Hint #9: The night before your bar mitzvah, get everything ready to go

And I mean everything. I'm talking underwear and socks. Lay it all out (OK, you might want to leave your suit or dress on a hanger), so that you can literally get out of bed and get dressed without using a single brain cell.

Set your own alarm. If you're worried about hearing it, then set two. Do not make someone else wake you up. Make a pile *ahead of time* of what you need to bring to temple. Folders. Prayer Books. *Tallit.* Breakfast? Put the cereal box and a bowl on the counter for yourself. (Leave the milk in the fridge.) Don't ask anyone to do anything for you that you can do yourself.

You should not have to remember or think about *anything* on the morning of your bar mitzvah.

Do you want to imagine the most wonderful sight in the world? The bar mitzvah kid, dressed, fed, sitting on the couch with the things that he needs, ten minutes before anyone needs to leave the house. Watch everyone go crazy, that's fine. You are golden. You'll have a perfect start to your bar mitzvah day.

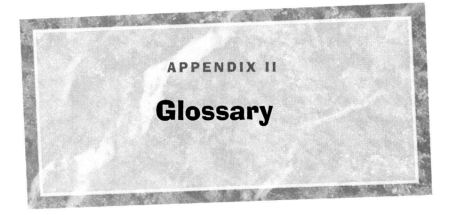

APPENDIX II

Glossary

Aliyah (pl. aliyot): The honor of being called up to the Torah. The person receiving an *aliyah* chants a short blessing before and after the Torah reading.

Amen: The response one makes after hearing a blessing. According to Jewish tradition, if you hear a blessing and say "amen," it's as if you recited the blessing yourself.

Amidah: "Standing prayer." The Amidah is the central part of every service, and is usually recited silently, and may be repeated again out loud by the cantor.

Amud: Podium or lectern on the bimah.

Aramaic: A language commonly spoken back in ancient times in the Middle East. It uses the same alphabet as Hebrew and shares many of the same roots.

Ark: In Hebrew, Aron Kodesh. Where the Torah scrolls are placed. It will usually be the central, most important location in the sanctuary.

Aron Kodesh: see Ark.

Ashrei: A prayer that is recited in the service, sometimes twice. The text is Psalm 145, and each line is in Hebrew alphabetical order.

Aufruf: The service before a wedding when the bride and groom are called up to the Torah for an *aliyah.* It commonly takes place on the Shabbat before the wedding.

Bar Mitzvah (pl. B'nei Mitzvah): "Son of the commandments." It describes a boy who has turned thirteen according to the Jewish calendar and is therefore now responsible to observe the Jewish laws and rituals.

Barchu: The public call to worship recited in each morning service. Can only be recited if there's a *minyan* present.

Bat Mitzvah (pl. B'not Mitzvah): "Daughter of the commandments." Same as *bar mitzvah,* but for a girl.

Bimah: The elevated area in front of the sanctuary where services are led. Sometimes referred to as the pulpit.

Birchot Hashachar: "Blessings of the morning." It is the opening section of every morning service.

Chumash: A book containing the text of the Torah. Also referred to as the Five Books of Moses.

Conservative: A branch of Judaism that follows traditional Jewish law but has made changes over the years to reflect modern society.

Daven: To pray (Yiddish).

D'var Torah: A short presentation explaining some text of the Torah or haftarah.

Egalitarian: Equal. Refers to a synagogue that allows the same observance and participation from males and females.

Five Books of Moses: see Torah.

G'lilah: The honor of dressing the Torah at the conclusion of the Torah service.

Haftarah (sometimes haftorah): The reading from one of the books of the Prophets that is linked to that week's Torah portion.

Hagbah: The honor of lifting the Torah at the conclusion of the Torah service.

Havdalah: The ceremony marking the conclusion of Shabbat on Saturday evening. It includes the use of wine (or grape juice), a special braided candle, and spices.

Hazzan: Cantor.

Honor: Any form of participation in the service by a member of the congregation. Many honors are concentrated around the Torah service, such as receiving an *aliyah* or performing *hagbah* and *g'lilah*.

Hosafah (pl. hosafot): "Additional." An extra *aliyah* (or *aliyot*) added to the usual seven on Shabbat.

Kaddish: A prayer, written in Aramaic, that praises God's name and appears in the service numerous times and in different forms. The most well-known version is the Mourners' Kaddish, recited after the death of a family member.

Kiddush: The prayer over wine (or grape juice).

Kislev: The Jewish month when Chanukah begins.

Kohen (pl. Kohanim): A descendant of the priestly class of Jews, who used to be in charge of the service in ancient Temple times.

Kosher: Adhering to specific dietary rules in Judaism. The most well-known rules are not mixing dairy with meat and the prohibition against pork and shellfish.

Levi (pl. Levi'im): A descendant of the Jewish tribe who used to be in charge of the care and maintentance of the ancient Temple, and who assisted the *Kohanim*.

Ma'ariv: Evening service.

Maftir: The *aliyah* following the usual seven on Shabbat. The person called up for this *aliyah* remains after the Torah reading to sing the haftarah.

Mezuzah (pl. mezuzot): A small case affixed to the doorpost of a Jewish home, which contains the first two paragraphs of the *Shema* written on a very small piece of parchment. This fulfills the commandment found in the *Shema* to "write these words on your gates and the doorposts of your home."

Mincha: Afternoon service.

Minyan: Ten or more adult Jews (must be of bar or bat mitzvah age or older).

Mitzvah (pl. mitzvot): Commandment. Sometimes refers to a good deed.

Motzi: The prayer over challah or other bread.

Mourners' Kaddish: see Kaddish.

Musaf: Additional service. It has to do with animal sacrifices that used to be offered in ancient Temple times.

Nisan: The Jewish month in which Passover takes place.

Orthodox: The branch of Judaism that strictly follows traditional Jewish law.

Parsha: The selection of Torah that is read on any given Shabbat. Sometimes also referred to as "sidrah."

Passover: Festival of spring when we eat only unleavened food.

Pesukei D'zimrah: "Verses of song." An early section of the morning service comprised mostly of Psalms.

Prophets (in Hebrew: Nevi'im): The section of the Bible that follows the Torah. This section is comprised of books that tell all about the ancient Israelite prophets and their messages.

Psalms: A book of the Bible that contains 150 separate poems or songs of praise to God.

Reform: The most liberal branch of Judaism, which does not believe that all traditional law is binding on today's Jews.

Rosh Chodesh: "Head of the month." The first day of the new Jewish month. Sometimes referred to as the New Moon.

Rosh Hashanah: "Head of the Year." The sacred Jewish holiday that marks the New Year.

Sanctuary: The room where services take place and the congregation worships. It contains the ark and the Torah scrolls.

Shabbat: The Jewish Sabbath. It begins at sundown on Friday evening and lasts until sundown on Saturday.

Shabbat Shalom: The traditional greeting which is said on Shabbat.

Shacharit: Morning service.

Shavuot: The holiday which commemorates God giving the Torah to the Jewish people. It falls in late May or early June.

Shema: The prayer which asserts that there is only One God. It is recited in every morning and evening service throughout the year.

Shiva: A period of mourning following the death of a family member. It is usually observed at home, traditionally for seven days.

Shmoneh Esrei (lit. "eighteen"): The Amidah.

Shochling: Swaying back and forth while praying. (Yiddish)

Shul: Synagogue. (Yiddish)

Siddur (pl. Siddurim): Prayer Book.

Simchat Torah: The holiday that celebrates the completion of the Torah, and beginning it all over again.

Sukkot: The holiday that recalls when the Israelites used to live in temporary structures throughout their years of wandering in the desert. It is also a festival that is tied to the fall harvest season.

Tallit (or tallis, pl. tallitot or taleisim): Prayer shawl worn during services.

Tallit katan: ("Small tallit"): A special kind of *tallit* worn under the clothing, not just for services but throughout the day.

Talmud: Volumes of Jewish teaching and discussion written two thousand years ago, when the Jewish people were living in Babylonia.

Tanakh: The Jewish Bible. The word is an acronym that stands for the three sections of the Bible—the Torah, Prophets, and Writings.

Tefilah (pl. tefilot): Prayer.

Tefillin: Small, black leather boxes and straps that are worn on the arm and head during a weekday morning service. Inside each box are excerpts from the Torah written on small pieces of parchment.

Temple: When written with a capital T, it refers to the Holy Temple that stood in Jerusalem about two thousand years ago and was the center of Jewish worship. It is now commonly used as another word for synagogue.

Three Festivals: Sukkot, Passover, and Shavuot.

Tikkun Olam ("Fixing the world"): The act of making the world a better place, which is the primary job of every Jewish person.

Tishrei: The first Jewish month of the year.

Torah: The first section of the Jewish Bible, consisting of the Five Books of Moses. The text is written on a large scroll that is housed in the ark.

Transliteration: Sounding out a Hebrew word using English letters.

Trope: The system of using symbols to determine how to sing the words of the Torah or haftarah. It is sometimes referred to as "cantillation."

Tzedakah: Charity.

Tzitzit: The fringes that are attached to each of the four corners of the *tallit*.

Writings (in Hebrew: Ketuvim): The third section of the Jewish Bible, which contains texts such as the Psalms, Proverbs, the Book of Esther, and other later books.

Yahrzeit: The anniversary of the day when a family member died.

Yiddish: A language spoken primarily by Jews and their descendants who lived in Europe. It is a combination mostly of German and Hebrew.

Yizkor: The memorial service recited four times a year, on each of the Three Festivals and Yom Kippur.

Yom Kippur: The Day of Atonement. It is the most sacred day in the Jewish calendar and takes place on the tenth day of the year, beginning with Rosh Hashanah.

Index

About the Author

Cantor Matt Axelrod has more than twenty years of experience teaching, coaching, prodding, and preparing students for the biggest day of their teenage years. A native of the Boston area, he is a graduate of Brandeis University and the Jewish Theological Seminary of America, and currently serves as cantor at Congregation Beth Israel in Scotch Plains, New Jersey. He is a past member of the Executive Council of the Cantors Assembly and a former president of its New Jersey Region, and has served on the United Synagogue Council on Jewish Education. Cantor Axelrod is also an avid aviation enthusiast as well as a licensed pilot and flight instructor who will occasionally promise kids an airplane ride as a bar mitzvah present.

For more tips on surviving your bar or bat mitzvah as well as your chance to join the discussion, please visit Cantor Axelrod's website at www.mattaxelrod.com.

**Are you interested in adopting this book for use
in your synagogue or Hebrew school?**

For information regarding discounts on bulk purchases, please contact

the Rowman & Littlefield Publishing Group
Special Sales Department:
special.sales@rowman.com

CPSIA information can be obtained at www.ICGtesting.com
Printed in the USA
BVOW040425260612

293586BV00001BA/1/P